WHALE MU

Three plays by

ANTHONY MINGHELLA

with an introduction by
Michael Coveney

WHALE MUSIC

A LITTLE LIKE DROWNING

TWO PLANKS AND A PASSION

A METHUEN PAPERBACK

A METHUEN NEW THEATRESCRIPT

First published in Great Britain as a paperback original in 1987 by Methuen London Ltd., 11 New Fetter Lane, London EC4P 4EE and in the United States of America by Methuen Inc., 29 West 35th Street, New York, NY 10001

Photoset in Times by 𝍅 Tek Art Limited, Croydon, Surrey

Printed in Great Britain by Richard Clay Ltd, Bungay, Suffolk

British Library Cataloguing in Publication Data

Minghella, Anthony
   Whale music and other plays.——(A Methuen
  new theatrescript).
  I. Title
  822'.914   PR6063.I4/

  ISBN 0-413-16700-3

'I know you're gonna think the water's a little brown, but you *can* drink it.'
from Woody Allen's 'Manhattan'

AUTHOR'S NOTE

In my experience, plays do not emerge, inevitable and finished, from the study. They are teased, cajoled and dragged into existence by producers, directors, friends and family. The plays in this collection are no exception and owe their appearance to a great many people. The catalogue of names which follows is by way of thanks to them all, not least Graeme, Johnny, Lou and – especially – Carolyn, who have never let me off and have never let me down.

WHALE MUSIC
University of Hull Drama Department. Jane Dale, Tina Perry, Eileen Ryan, Alison Watt and Alison Head. Jim Hawkins, Pedr James, Howard Baker, Vanessa Whitburn.

A LITTLE LIKE DROWNING
Caroline Hunt, Rod Lewis, Lee and Pam Elliott, Warren Hooper, Michael Attenborough, John Dove and Alfredo Molina.

TWO PLANKS AND A PASSION
Harry Thompson, Alan Strachan, Danny Boyle, Robert Cooper.

For brevity's sake, only cast lists from the first stage productions of each play have been included. This does no justice to subsequent companies, often working in other media, whose insights and skills have registered on the published texts.

Anthony Minghella
Highgate, 1987

CONTENTS

INTRODUCTION

The three plays in this volume form a good introduction to a writer who defies categorisation and critical pigeonholes. Anthony Minghella was born and raised on the Isle of Wight, comes of Anglo-Italian stock, has lectured in drama at Hull University, has been attached to both the Royal Court and the Tricycle Theatres in London, served as a script editor on *Grange Hill*, the excellent TV series about life in a London comprehensive school, and has spread his work around all of the available media except, so far, the cinema.

Although his first full-length play was produced at the end of the 1970s, *Whale Music*, which was premièred in Hull in 1980 and directed for Granada TV by Pedr James three years later, was the first to attract wide attention. Set in an unspecified coastal resort in the South of England, it combines two of Minghella's key preoccupations – time cycles ruled by the sea, and issues of maternity in tight domestic situations – with a brave and successful attempt to write about contemporary feminine consciousness.

Caroline, the central character in *Whale Music*, has taken time out of university to have a baby. Her friends gather round, first to support her, and second to define the experience in relation to their own lives. As in *Lysistrata* or some recent work of playwrights like Sarah Daniels and Caryl Churchill, Minghella's world excludes men, yet is no more 'imagined' than the stage worlds of his feminist peers.

As a male dramatist, Minghella is surprisingly unafraid to articulate the landlady Stella's torrential avenging rage against his own species; or to make Fran's defence of the family and traditional social values sound less reasonable than pious. The devotion of Caroline's old English teacher is also touchingly handled, as is the portrait of a disaffected teenage lesbian whom the teacher brings down to the coast with her. Nor does Minghella flinch from allowing Caroline to define her own heterosexual ache in a remarkable bedroom scene in which the teacher offers to bring up the child with Caroline.

In the end, the child is whisked away by unseen adoptive parents, establishing another Minghella theme that he developed more intricately in his Channel 4 trilogy *What If It's Raining?* (1986). Admittedly skirting the question of custody, this picture of a young father, deprived of his child by a failed marriage and emerging from social trauma to find new sexual partners, approached the subject of childbirth and parental care from the opposite direction to that in *Whale Music*. There is talk in both works of 'the family bed', of extending the protective womb into the habit of family bed-sharing.

Sex and family life are subjected to a different focusing method in *A Little Like Drowning* (1982), a snapshot memorial play of shimmering emotional density spanning three generations of Italian Catholics. Minghella's next stage work after *Whale Music*, it, too, is a series of coastal disturbances, the grandmother Leonora re-living her phoney marriage to opera-loving Alfredo in the company of her granddaughter on a grey English beach.

This is one of two plays in which Minghella has drawn directly on his own family history (the other, *Love Bites*, was produced at the Derby Playhouse in 1984). The action is flecked with instances of Catholic ritual: the display of a wedding-night sheet, a visit to the opera, a raucous wedding party, a last ditch confession by the adulterous Alfredo. But all these events are exposed as fraudulent, as visibly hypocritical signs of the contradictory spiritual reality. In performance, an intriguing tension is set up between the reminiscence of Leonora and the earth-larding virility of the husband who left her with three girls for 'that puttana'. But the framing device of recollection allows Leonora her revenge by claiming Alfredo's corpse to lie next to hers in eternity.

A Little Like Drowning is an unusual, beguiling play that relies for its fragrance of authenticity not on its details of place (these are negligible, apart from the overriding vistas of sea and sky) or even of time, but for the immaculacy of its light comedy and quirkily intimate confessional style. Just as Leonora never saw her husband naked, so we hear of Alfredo's account to her of their daughter's beauty when spied in the bathroom: like a bud opening.

The fact that Alfredo is a dealer in amusement machines turned, in later life, bingo caller is less relevant to Minghella's purpose than his passion for Puccini and Caruso. After the emotional complexities of *Whale Music* and *A Little Like Drowning*, the third play collected here is further evidence of Minghella's variety and range of interests. *Two Planks and a Passion*, technically ingenious and thoroughly entertaining, is at first sight an oddly remote project. We are in York in 1392 as the guilds prepare for the performance of their Mystery play on the feast of Corpus Christi.

As they do so, Richard II arrives in the city with his beloved, doomed Anne of Bohemia, and his playful best friend, the Earl of Oxford. The Mayor and the Master of the Painter's Guild, Geoffrey Le Kolve, and their respective wives, seek royal favour through the offer of hospitality and the local entertainment. But the plays are threatened with economic cuts (a time when there were *four* soldiers in the crucifixion scene is wistfully recalled), best bits have been 'hacked off as a saving' and there is general despair as to how the correct impression might be made with a fuzz-faced Mary and a fat Christ.

Minghella's stylistic idiom is a cunning mix of low crudity and heightened vernacular, itself based in the language of the Mystery Plays. The impulses behind the fawning instinct to present a play for approval and social ingratiation have literary antecedents in Shakespeare and Gogol; but what Minghella is creating, in a typically oblique and modest way, is a dramatic analogue, disguised as an historical tapestry, for many aspects and obsessions of today's theatre community.

Two Planks is about patronage and subsidy, fascinatingly poised between the historical plight of a politically beleaguered King, 'sullen with London', in holiday mood, and the bright actuality of artists under the hammer. The new realism of the Mysteries is bemoaned by the priest who, if it was up to him, would never show Christ wounded; 'but the taste is for mumbling and hurt and violence and cruelty.' Vain efforts are made to beef up the Herod play with exploding bags of blood and exotic masks while the royal party interpose a new realism of their own in the King's invention of 'wipes' for nose and bum (Minghella is mindful that 'handkerchief' does not enter the language for another 140 odd years) and Bohemia's oddly endearing fetish for luxuriant beds.

We also witness the evolution of sporting fashion with Richard insisting that the Mayor's croquet lawn be dug for golf, rendering the official's sward 'a veritable sieve.' The game itself, strewn with cringing denials of victory, is the most visceral, enjoyable onstage ball game since Edward Bond's cricket match in *The Pope's Wedding*.

All three of these plays have been re-written and re-worked through various productions and media. One senses that this ongoing process is part and parcel of Minghella's practical and pragmatic approach to his craft. As my brief career outline may have indicated, he is, refreshingly, not above mixing it with popular television values.

What If It's Raining? was a Channel 4 film with a snowbound *Kramer v Kramer* mood about it and a marked similarity to the smarter, slicker collaboration between Christopher Hampton and novelist Peter Prince in another Channel 4 film, *The Good Father*. The main difference was that, in the latter, Anthony Hopkins's grizzled lonely divorcee was very much older than Michael Maloney's beautifully observed and inflected young father. Minghella's voice is that of a man honestly documenting the range of his own experience between late adolescence and early middle age.

His refusal to speculate in emotional matters is all the more impressive in his latest full-length stage play, already published by Methuen, *Made in Bangkok* (1986). The sexual and marital dilemmas of his heroine on the 'Eastern Promise' package trip to Thailand are convincingly and movingly enacted on the brink of middle age while juvenile excess and macho strutting are fatuously indulged in the neon-lit bars and massage parlours of an unreal, manufactured environment.

Made in Bangkok is obviously energised by its being, in the first place, a study of a group outing, a random collective dislocated from home territory; each of the tourists, in different ways, is both liberated by the experience and confined by an inability to handle it. Some of Minghella's work is derived from a collaborative workshop methodology, which is why, presumably, he writes so effectively about molecular cell-like structures, be they the interdependent society of *Whale Music*, the explosive non-nuclear family in *A Little Like Drowning*, the industrial hierarchy of pinners, painters, merchants and royalty in *Two Planks and a Passion*, or the holidaymakers in *Made in Bangkok*.

This anthology shows the creative evolution of one of the most distinctive yet unclassifiable new dramatists to emerge in the 1980s. He is not knowing or overtly witty, like Hampton or Hare; nor is he a scabrous rabble-rouser like Barker or Brenton; nor is he an educated polemicist like Griffiths or Edgar. He is his own man with a will to work, a tendency to experiment, a talent both to surprise and amuse, and a great propensity to keep audiences – and critics – guessing as to what might come next.

Above all, he is not anxious to patent the sound of his own voice in the way that dramatists such as John Whiting and Christopher Fry have done in the past; that day may yet come.

For the moment, what some might diagnose a fatal lack of identifiable *personality* as a dramatist is in fact submerged beneath something much more interesting – the indecipherable babble, almost, of thought, character and action sprouting from deep-rooted obsessions with community, parenthood, love and duty. It will do to be going on with.

Michael Coveney, 1987

WHALE MUSIC

For Hannah

Whale Music was written for students at the University of Hull Drama Department in June 1980. It received its first professional production at the Haymarket Theatre, Leicester in April 1981, with the following cast:

CAROLINE	Michele Copsey
STELLA	Carol Leader
FRAN	Camille Davis
KATE	Julie Legrand
D	Sadie Hamilton
VERONICA	Mary Waterhouse
WAITRESS	
SHEELAGH O'BRIEN	Anne Jameson

Directed by Colin George

Setting: the Isle of Wight.
Time: the present.

This version of the play includes a NURSE and STAFF NURSE.

ACT ONE

Scene One

STELLA's *Flat. Winter.*
  CAROLINE *has answered* STELLA's
advertisement for a lodger. STELLA *shows
her the room.*

STELLA: This is it. Not enormous.

CAROLINE (*not looking at the room
  much; checking the window*): No, it's
  fine. Do you want a deposit? I can write
  you a cheque.

STELLA: The wardrobe's full, I'm afraid.
  I'll clear it out tomorrow.

CAROLINE: That's OK. I don't have
  much with me.

STELLA: I use this as a dark room in the
  summer. There's a blind. Great if you're
  into meditation.

CAROLINE *goes to the window.*

CAROLINE: The sea.

STELLA: Oh yeah. It's everywhere. The
  gulls will probably keep you awake at
  first. You'll get used to them. They
  scream at the weather.

CAROLINE: I was born here.

STELLA: Oh. That makes sense. You're
  either born in this place or you come
  here to die. Listen, you couldn't manage
  cash, could you? A cheque's a bit . . .

CAROLINE: Of course.

STELLA: Just, I don't work in the winter.
  I sign on as a beach photographer. But
  the facts of life don't interest Social
  Security much. They think it's my fault
  that nobody sunbathes in November.
  But they DO pay the rent and they
  wouldn't like it if they found out you
  did too. As it is I keep getting visits from
  unpleasant men before breakfast,
  demanding to examine the mattress for
  signs of cohabitation. Which is pretty
  absurd. However high in protein sperm's
  supposed to be, it can hardly amount
  to dependency. I keep telling them it
  would never stand up in court. Did you
  tell me your name?

CAROLINE: It's Caroline.

STELLA: I'm Stella. Listen, forget the
  deposit – but you can give me a week's
  rent in advance if you like.

CAROLINE: Thanks. Oh – is there a
  bathroom?

STELLA: Yeah. It's downstairs. If you
  want hot water there's a meter – 10ps –
  you have to kick the coinbox. (*She takes
  the rent.*) Great. If anyone asks, I'm
  going to say you're an old school friend
  come to stay. Is that OK?

CAROLINE: Yes, that's fine.

STELLA: Tremendous. (*She offers her
  hand.*) Good to see you, old school
  friend.

Pause.

Anything wrong?

CAROLINE: No. (*Pause.*) Why?
  (*Pause.*)

STELLA: Hey, do you cook?

CAROLINE: A little.

STELLA: A girl who cooks! I cook tins
  and packets. Oh – and I can thaw frozen
  things.

CAROLINE: I reheat take-aways.

STELLA: Never touch them. I'm working
  hard at getting anorexia.

CAROLINE: Why's that?

STELLA: Oh, it's the fashion to be
  unhealthy. Anyone who's anyone looks
  as if they could do with a good square
  meal. I've never lived with another girl
  before. When you moving in?

CAROLINE: Now?

STELLA: I'll make some tea.

CAROLINE: Uh – no thanks.

STELLA: Coffee? Booze?

CAROLINE: No, I'm fine. But don't let
  me stop you.

STELLA: Is it a man?

CAROLINE: Is what a man?

STELLA: Why you're here?

CAROLINE: No.

STELLA: Sorry. I know. I ask too many
  questions.

CAROLINE: No. Depends what kind of
  reply you want. How are you? – fine –
  or, how are you? – falling apart, suicidal.
  You know – polite or honest. I'm fine
  on the polite.

STELLA: It's cold in here. I hate the winter. I try not to go outside. The idea is to raid a supermarket in September and lock the door until April. Go in a slug; emerge a butterfly.

CAROLINE: What do you do?

STELLA: Paint. No. Plan paintings. Think about them. In fact, nothing much. I mean preferably I find a man to lock in with me. Else I go maudlin. On balance I've been better off maudlin. I set one loose yesterday. There was something VERY wrong with him. He's left a smell. Did you notice? Musty. he's gone off to find a cave in Greece.

CAROLINE: Really?

STELLA: My dear, this is the dregs of the beautiful people you're moving in with. You know: record collection stops at Hendrix. South coast trying hard to be West coast. Marijuana and muesli.

CAROLINE: You don't sound very convinced.

STELLA: It pales like everything else. How long do you plan to stay?

CAROLINE: I don't know. Until the Spring.

STELLA: A fellow hibernator.

CAROLINE: Oh yes.

STELLA: There are some things I can't work out.

CAROLINE: Yes?

STELLA: Strictly polite questions. Like why not stay with parents? Where school friends?

CAROLINE: Easy. Parents not here. Moved to Derbyshire. School friend here. Has family. I want to see her but I wouldn't want to stay. I'd trip all over the acquisitions.

STELLA: I see. And what – have you been at college or something?

CAROLINE: Yes. Leeds. I'm taking a year off. That's my speciality. I took a year off before I went, too.

STELLA: Good?

CAROLINE: My year off? No. Well good, yes, to have . . . to get around. That was good. The bits in between were on the whole not good. At all.

STELLA: Where d'you go?

CAROLINE: Most places on the Underground, Islington the longest.

STELLA: Funny – you left here and went to London. With me it was the reverse. I came down here for a festival and never left.

CAROLINE: It's the air.

STELLA: It's laziness. Nobody minds here. It's a lazy place. If you give up in London, half the caring agencies in the world are fighting over you. Compared to the noise those vultures make, the seagulls sound terrific.

CAROLINE: I'm going to walk and walk and walk.

STELLA (unimpressed): Wonderful.

CAROLINE: We used to hate tourists. Grockles, we called them. Armies of little fat red people in vests collapsing on the beach, wobbling into the water. When I think of the Summer that's all I see. Now you can shoot a gun down the high street. You can walk for hours. You can breathe a bit. I want to get my lungs full. Throw some stones.

STELLA: Well, don't worry about me. I won't clutter up the landscape. I'll wobble about here. You haven't got a thing about mice, have you?

CAROLINE: No. Why?

STELLA: They've moved in too. I think the Greek god must have brought them with him. I went to make my toast this morning and it looked like a Polo mint.

CAROLINE: Perhaps you'd better get a trap or something.

STELLA: I've got a trap. I've got two traps. I've also got poison and I'm thinking of getting an air rifle. I tell you – it's them or me.

CAROLINE: A cat's more effective. (She eyes Stella.) You don't like cats.

STELLA: At least mice just nick food. Cats expect you to buy them the stuff. I adopted a cat once. I thought it was dying or something. I'm bloody certain it gave me worms. And it stank. AND it was permanently on heat. Hey, are you sure you're all right?

CAROLINE: It's nothing. I just feel a bit tired. I'll be OK in a second. Could I have some water?

CAROLINE *lies down on the bed. She suddenly retches and scrabbles for a tissue in her bag.*

CAROLINE: Oh. I'm sorry. Oh.

STELLA: Hey, don't die on me.

CAROLINE: I'm really sorry.

STELLA: Listen, have you seen a doctor?

CAROLINE: Yes. Thanks. I feel much better.

STELLA: Well, what did he say?

CAROLINE: It's a she and she said I was pregnant.

Scene Two

A café.
CAROLINE *is sitting at a table stirring coffee.* FRAN *enters, 'Clothkits' to the nines, carrying a couple of carrier bags.*

FRAN (*with genuine pleasure*): Hello!

FRAN *and* CAROLINE *embrace.*

CAROLINE (*with genuine pleasure*): Hello!

FRAN (*breathlessly*): I'm really sorry I'm late. I've had heaps to do. Absolutely mad. And I forgot to put the timer on the casserole. Do you know I haven't been to this cafe since, years, since school. It's great.

CAROLINE (*delighted*): It's awful. Where's Heidi?

FRAN: At mum's.

CAROLINE: What a shame. I'm dying to see her.

FRAN: Oh yes. She's a terror. Honestly, she's a real scream. She's crawling.

CAROLINE: Really.

FRAN: You should see the house. She can destroy a room in five minutes. She tried to eat the liquidiser this morning.

CAROLINE: Let me get you a cup of tea.

FRAN: Please. I'm parched. This is lovely.

Five minutes peace.

CAROLINE: Could we have two teas, please? (*To Fran.*) You hungry?

FRAN: I'd love a scone or something.

CAROLINE: And a scone, please.

FRAN: Well. I got your letter.

CAROLINE: Good.

FRAN: I think you're really brave. I really do.

CAROLINE: Oh Fran.

FRAN: No really. I mean if Heidi had come along and I hadn't been . . . What I mean to say is that so many girls, you know . . . just take the easy way out.

CAROLINE: I didn't know there was an easy way out. If there had been I would have grabbed it.

FRAN: No, I know, of course. And you look so well. I went all blotchy and cow-like and my hair fell out in chunks.

CAROLINE: I feel terrible.

FRAN: Oh love.

CAROLINE: I'm getting morning, afternoon and evening sickness.

FRAN: Ah, it'll be a girl. Have you done the needle test?

CAROLINE: What?

FRAN: Dangle a needle over your lump. It works. If it goes up and down it's a boy, and if it goes round and round in circles its a girl. It's something to do with electricity.

A WAITRESS *brings tea and a scone. She is not a happy waitress.*

CAROLINE: Thanks.

FRAN: Let me get this.

WAITRESS: You pay at the counter.

The WAITRESS *goes.*

FRAN: I know her. You know who she is, don't you? She was in the third year when we were prefects. She was Maureen thing's friend – the one who pushed drugs.

CAROLINE: Is it? Anyway, you do exaggerate, Fran. She told you she'd smoked a joint once.

FRAN: Well. Do you know who else I saw recently? Launa Carter. Vast. Like the side of a house. She was a size eight in the sixth form. Poor thing. She looked really depressed. Do you see anyone?

CAROLINE: No. Just you.

FRAN: How's Miss Lawrence?

CAROLINE: OK. Don't call her Miss Lawrence, Fran. She doesn't teach us any more.

FRAN: I know. But I can't think of her as Kate, somehow. It seems blasphemous.

CAROLINE: Well don't call her Miss Lawrence when you see her. She'll have a fit.

FRAN: Why, is she here?

CAROLINE: No. Not yet. But she will be.

FRAN: Really?

CAROLINE: Don't know. She's coming for my birthday, definitely.

FRAN: That will be nice. She's so fond of you, isn't she? That must have been great when she got the job in Leeds.

CAROLINE: Yes, it was.

FRAN: I didn't realize you were actually sharing together.

CAROLINE: It's Kate's house. I just have a room.

FRAN: It's amazing how things work out. You couldn't have guessed, could you, that you'd both end up in Leeds together?

CAROLINE: And you a mum.

FRAN: Oh, come on, I was marked down as a breeder from the word go. All my brains are in my womb.

CAROLINE: Rubbish.

FRAN: It's true. When Heidi appeared, something in me went click. Into overdrive. (*Pause.*) I'm sorry Caroline, we're talking babies. I promised myself I wouldn't. She's got Graeme's hair. Not that she's got much.

CAROLINE: How is Graeme?

FRAN: Busy. He's fine. In and out like a maniac. They've made him a partner. Can you imagine? He wears a suit!

CAROLINE: Amazing.

FRAN: He said to say Hello.

CAROLINE: Say hello back.

FRAN: Right. (*Pause.*) I've brought you some things. Don't be insulted. Everything's so expensive.

CAROLINE: Stupid. What sort of things?

FRAN: Here. There's a couple of sleep bras. You'll need those. And a really nice smock and trouser thing from Clothkits. The trousers have an elasticated waist so they grow with you.

CAROLINE: You're a dear, Fran. Bless you. (*She looks in the bag. What she sees upsets her.*) Thank you.

FRAN: I hope I'll have to ask for them back soon. (*Quietly.*) Oh, Caroline. Why don't you come and stay with us? We'd love to have you. I'd be ever so useful – I'm encyclopaedic about pregnancy.

CAROLINE: I'm not good company just now. But thanks.

FRAN: Think about it. It's an open invitation. It would be nice to have a grown-up around.

CAROLINE: Grown-up! Anyway, doesn't Graeme qualify?

FRAN: When he's in. It's hard for men. They don't get so excited by feeds and nappies. And I believe in the family bed.

CAROLINE: The what? No, don't tell me. Heidi sleeps with the two of you. Right?

FRAN: You disapprove.

CAROLINE: Not at all. It's not my business.

FRAN: Graeme says it's ridiculous. But I think it'll make so much difference later on. Besides, it's marvellous. We all cuddle up and she can help herself if she gets hungry in the night.

CAROLINE: Yes, but what about you and Graeme?

FRAN: What about us?

CAROLINE: I mean, what if you have a second baby?

The WAITRESS *comes forward.*

WAITRESS: We're closing.

FRAN: Sorry. (*She devours the scone.*) Mmm. Just the job. (*Pause.*) It's so nice to see you again.

CAROLINE: Good old Fran. Constant as ever.

FRAN: What d'you mean?

CAROLINE: Nothing. It's just good to see you too.

FRAN: I'm a twit. I almost forgot. Two special pressies. (*She produces a record.*) Now, this is wonderful.

CAROLINE (*reading the back of the record sleeve*): Whale Music?

FRAN: Yes, they sing to each other. It's ever so strange. What you do is play it and relax. It's supposed to comfort the baby.

CAROLINE: Ta.

FRAN: No, really. It's tremendous. It's like being very deep under water. Womb-like.

CAROLINE: But it's already in the womb.

FRAN: Well, Heidi loved it. And there's simulated heart beats and things and some Purcell. Only that side's a bit scratched.

CAROLINE: I'll play it, I promise.

FRAN (*holding up a book*): And there's this. '*Essential exercises for the child-bearing year*'.

CAROLINE: Oh God, Fran.

FRAN: They're a must, Caroline. Otherwise you'll look like a deflated balloon afterwards. And it makes such a difference for your labour. Don't make that face. It's going to happen. It's no use pretending it won't.

CAROLINE: Fran, do you think we could change the subject for a minute?

FRAN: Oh, sugar! I'm sorry. I know, I'm like a steamroller when I get going. That's what Graeme says. I'm sorry love. Do you want to go for a walk? You must walk a lot.

CAROLINE: I'd like to go down to the beach.

FRAN: Lovely. You sit there and I'll pay this.

CAROLINE, *alone for a second, gathers up the things. She inspects them.*

FRAN (*to the* WAITRESS): It was a lovely scone. (*To* CAROLINE.) I wish I'd brought Heidi now. She loves sand. And you wouldn't have minded, would you?

CAROLINE: Of course not.

FRAN: I thought she might have upset you.

CAROLINE: Nobody's going to die, Fran.

FRAN: I know, I know. It's just I know how I'd feel.

CAROLINE: I feel like there's glass in my guts. That's all. Everything else is just numb.

FRAN: Well, I'm sure a walk will do you good.

WAITRESS: D'you think you might hurry up?

FRAN: I shouldn't bother with the Clearasil. It just joins the spots together.

CAROLINE: Oh Fran!

FRAN: Want to hear the noise the whales make? It's like this . . . (*She makes whale noises.*)

The WAITRESS *stacks chairs on table.*

WAITRESS (*to an unseen partner*): D'you know her trouble? The husband goes up every skirt in the town . . . except hers.

Scene Three

STELLA's *Flat.*

CAROLINE *and* FRAN *are doing an essential exercise for the child-bearing year.* STELLA *is in a chair, smoking and drinking.* FRAN *reads aloud an instruction from the manual.*

STELLA: That thing in there will be mentally disturbed by the time it drops out. It probably won't ever come out now. You can see it thinking bugger that, mate, if it's this bad in the padded cell you can forget the great outdoors.

CAROLINE: Stella's right This is killing me. What about my twenty minutes total relaxation, Fran?

FRAN: Once more.

CAROLINE: Once more.

FRAN: Come on. Big effort. (*She yells out instructions.*)

STELLA: I know what it is. It's the Karma Sutra done single-handed.

CAROLINE (*laughing*): I think I'm breaking something.

FRAN: That's good!

STELLA: That's good, Caroline. Break something!

CAROLINE: Oh come on, Stella. It's great for the anorexia.

STELLA: So's dying. (*Getting up.*) This bloody rain will drive me crazy. Who's for a drink?

FRAN *and* CAROLINE *loll about, exhausted.*

FRAN: I've brought some Lucozade. Do you fancy some, Caroline?

CAROLINE (*laughing*): I do, actually.

STELLA: Terrific!

FRAN: Your day will come. Have you got a boyfriend?

STELLA: Oh yeah. He's in the wardrobe right now. I keep him in kit form. No, my day won't come. I don't have Caroline's scruples.

FRAN: Oh, I don't know. I think you might feel different if it happened. You see – well, this is my theory anyway – it's not just a question of giving house-room to an egg for a few months . . . no, all kinds of things – hormones and what have you – are rushing about, sort of educating you for motherhood. It's very animal, I think. I mean, it's like the way your milk suddenly comes, for instance.

CAROLINE (*bitterly*): Where does that leave me?

STELLA: Right.

FRAN: Well, I don't know. I don't know, but it's love I'm talking about really, isn't it? I mean, I don't think that can hurt you.

STELLA: Oh! Come on!

FRAN: I think Caroline knows what I mean.

CAROLINE: No, I don't.

FRAN: I wish I hadn't started this.

STELLA: It strikes me, Fran, you wouldn't have a problem if it came up and bit you. Well, love's great. I hear you can buy it from Habitat.

FRAN *looks to* CAROLINE.

CAROLINE: Don't look at me. I lose both ways, don't I? Do you know, when I told my mother what had happened, she said, 'Only a whore would sleep in two men's beds'. No, not 'sleep in' – 'go to' – those were her words. 'Only a whore would go to two men's beds.' She was in the garden, pruning roses. She had a pair of those secateur things in her hand. She didn't look at me, she stared at the roses and told me it would kill my father. I know she didn't mean it. Basically she's kind. But those are the words that stick. Anyway, then we went indoors and everybody cried and then . . . then we had a cup of tea.

There is a pause.

FRAN: You haven't drunk your Lucozade.

STELLA: I didn't realize there were two men involved.

CAROLINE: Oh, yes.

STELLA: Have you told them?

CAROLINE: They both think the other is the father. It seemed simplest.

FRAN: I think you're right. Tell a man he's going to be a father and you burst a door marked hero.

STELLA: You're really sold on the metaphysics, aren't you?

FRAN: I've seen it in action.

STELLA: Well I don't know if it's such a good idea. Why should they get off?

CAROLINE: I don't want to see them.

STELLA: Bugger seeing them. What about money? What about a bit of moral support? Why should you have to cope by yourself?

CAROLINE: I'm not. I'm here.

STELLA: What kind of set-up is this? What is it when we're all clucking about like hens with our Lucozade and knitting and sticking our bloody bums in the air? Can you see a man doing that?

FRAN: Are you saying you think men ought to have more to do with their families? Because if that's what you mean you don't know them. Have you seen men with babies? It's laughable. I think it's a crime to leave a child with a man.

CAROLINE: Come off it, Fran.

STELLA: That's just crap.

FRAN: Is it? I'm sorry. I wouldn't go out to work and leave Heidi with Graeme. I wouldn't trust him. They push prams – have you watched them? You'd think they were walking on nails. His idea of playing with Heidi is to sit her in the playroom and watch her through the newspaper. That's why it's a woman's job. Because men can't do it.

STELLA: You mean WON'T do it.

FRAN: No. It's just not in them with all the will in the world. A child goes to its mother. You don't have to tell it.

STELLA: What do you expect? Your husband isn't wearing milk bottles, is he?

FRAN: No, he isn't. And I don't think that's an accident.

CAROLINE: I don't think you believe it. But if you say it often enough you can live with it.

FRAN: Because it's always been that way doesn't make it wrong. Just unfashionable.

STELLA: Just bollocks.

FRAN: No! I'm sick and tired of women telling me I'm wasting my life. Envy thy husband's penis. No. I'm sorry. You have to cut it off now, don't you? There is something that neither of you can understand. You talk about love, Stella – you've got no idea – because it's not love, you're right. It's not love with men and women, it's necessity. Love is between the mother and her child. That's why you're so poisoned. That's why men work so hard at making everything else look more fulfilling, because it's not their magic, it's my magic. And what's so sad, is that women are abandoning what they have because they think men are hiding some miracle in their hands. But there's no miracle . . . This is it, you see there's no miracle.

STELLA: I've got to hand it to you – you can't be all bad if you hate men that much.

FRAN: I didn't mean to say I hated men. Is that what it sounds like?

STELLA: Maybe it's just your husband. I think you had him up against the wall there – along with me and the liberated lesbians.

CAROLINE: You didn't say lesbians.

FRAN: No, I didn't. Did you say there was a drink going? I've finished this.

STELLA: That's more like it, have a proper drink, that stuff will rot your teeth.

FRAN: I was just thinking – I was beginning to sound like a grudging hausfrau.

STELLA: You were – and so what? A little grudge never hurt anyone. Which is more than can be said for hausfrauing.

FRAN: You get into this circle. Babies and mothers and your mothers and baby-sitting circles and, you know, magazines and double-drainers, like – that's a good example – do you know I was the only wife in the Close without a double drainer and it got to me so much I couldn't get to sleep thinking about it. But what I'm saying is, in that circle, well, no-one talks about anything really, I mean you'd think to listen to us that nobody got depressed or frustrated. I mean, I'm not even talking about the bloody world, about a single bloody current event, I'm talking about our own lives. Not a murmur. It's like it's some dreadful treachery to admit you're fed up. And then someone turns up to a coffee morning and in the middle of what's new in Mothercare says, 'By the way, we're getting divorced' and bursts into tears. (*Pause.*) That actually happened.

There is a pause.

CAROLINE: In Leeds nobody talks about anything BUT themselves or orgasms, or Women Against Rape or, I don't know, Nicaragua, and I don't see that doing much to alleviate the general misery.

STELLA: This is awful! God! I think I preferred the exercises. In a minute we'll all be lying on the ground wailing, which reminds me – the whale record – wow!

FRAN: Oh, do you like it?

STELLA: No, it's absolutely horrendous, but it's got rid of the mice!

CAROLINE: Stella rigged up the stereo in the kitchen.

STELLA: They ran up the street waving white flags.

FRAN: It's not that bad.

STELLA imitates whale music.

CAROLINE: I'd like to go out.

STELLA: It's raining.

CAROLINE: I don't mean the beach. I mean US go out.

FRAN: Where?

CAROLINE: I don't know. What about a disco?

STELLA: You want to go dancing?

CAROLINE: I do. Come on, Fran, we could take the exercises.

FRAN: I haven't been to a disco since, oh, I don't know. Can't remember.

CAROLINE: Right. Where do we go? You're the expert Stella.

STELLA: At this time of year? There might be a late funeral.

CAROLINE: Boring. So where were you on Saturday?

STELLA: The Sixty-nine.

CAROLINE: What's wrong with that?

STELLA: We can't go there. It's really nasty. Besides, it's not a disco, it's a cattle market.

CAROLINE: We could ignore all that and just have a dance.

STELLA: Around our bags?

FRAN: I can't. I ought to get back.

CAROLINE: I thought Heidi was sleeping at your mum's.

FRAN: No, but Graeme will be there. The football club always go for a drink after training.

CAROLINE: Great. You can dance with Graeme.

STELLA: And we'll have the football club.

CAROLINE: That's settled then.

FRAN: What if he's dancing with someone else?

STELLA: I would think it's pretty unlikely he WON'T be dancing with someone else.

FRAN: I know.

STELLA: Well, look love, I've never met your husband but it strikes me it wouldn't hurt to remind him that you can wiggle your udders with the best of them.

FRAN: You're right. You've never met him.

CAROLINE: Well, OK, let's go somewhere else.

FRAN: No. We'll go there. Sod him. Can I borrow something to wear?

STELLA: A holster?

FRAN: Hmm. It's dangerous, isn't it? Talk – I mean, women talking. If we ever had a union the world would stop dead.

STELLA: Well, it certainly puts a whole new light on withdrawing labour.

CAROLINE groans.

FRAN: I'm enjoying this. I'm really enjoying myself.

Scene Four

STELLA's Flat. Morning.
CAROLINE is alone, going through a bundle of letters and a parcel. She is wearing a dressing gown.
STELLA enters, dressed as the previous scene but rather the worse for wear.

STELLA: Oh, you're up.

CAROLINE: D'you want coffee?

STELLA: No.

CAROLINE makes a point of going through the letters.

OK, I know what you're thinking.

CAROLINE: Do you?

STELLA: Look, have you got any money?

CAROLINE: Yes.

STELLA: I need a cigarette and a shower.

CAROLINE: I'll get my purse.

STELLA: We can take it off the rent.

CAROLINE: I've paid the rent.

CAROLINE *exits for her purse and returns immediately.*

STELLA: Next week's then. How did you get home?

CAROLINE: I walked.

STELLA: What happened to Fran?

CAROLINE: They left. I didn't hear what was said. But the headlines were plain enough.

STELLA: Not good.

CAROLINE: No.

STELLA: Well, it's her own fault. What did she expect?

CAROLINE: It's our fault. We should have gone somewhere else. We shouldn't have gone at all.

STELLA: That why you didn't stay?

CAROLINE: I was by myself.

STELLA: Not when I started dancing.

CAROLINE: Oh no, not then – then I was being massaged by a psychopath.

STELLA: I thought that's what you went for.

CAROLINE: I thought I was going out with you and Fran. Anyway, let's forget it. (*Pointed.*) How was YOUR night?

STELLA: Oh, piss off.

CAROLINE (*looking in her purse*): Will five pounds do, Stella? (*Pause. Then, thawing.*) You don't have to feel guilty.

STELLA: No, I don't have to. Do you feel OK?

CAROLINE (*smiling*): Awful.

STELLA (*smiling*): Me too.

CAROLINE (*pointing to the parcel*): From my mother. Red Cross parcel. I've just eaten a pound bar of fruit and nut. I saved you a piece.

STELLA (*accepting it and sitting down*): I don't know why I did it. Reflex. Didn't even fancy him. D'you know what he does? You won't believe this – he works for Social Security.

CAROLINE (*laughing*): Was he on duty?

STELLA: He was barely conscious. Stupid, isn't it? But it was raining and he had a car, and I didn't fancy walking home much. And then, of course, this morning it's still raining and I had even further to walk. (*She sighs.*) I must have a shower. (*Looking at the pile of letters and the parcels.*) Someone's popular.

CAROLINE: Stella. Graeme . . .

STELLA: What about him?

CAROLINE: You know him, don't you?

STELLA: Yes, probably. It's a small place. I know everyone.

CAROLINE: That's not what I meant. I don't think it was reflex that made you go off so suddenly.

STELLA (*sighing*): I know him.

CAROLINE: I knew it – what a joke.

STELLA: I didn't find it funny.

CAROLINE: You've slept with him. Right?

STELLA: Yes, I've slept with him.

CAROLINE: So've I. So have I.

STELLA (*astounded*): When?

CAROLINE: That's pretty funny, isn't it? He was the first. When we were at school.

STELLA: Oh. Does Fran know?

CAROLINE: No.

STELLA: Well, you live and learn.

CAROLINE: You certainly do.

STELLA: Has he changed much?

CAROLINE: Look it was a farce – the whole thing. It was just . . . I don't know what it was.

STELLA: I just can't see it. You.

CAROLINE: It has happened. (*Referring to her stomach.*) Very much so.

STELLA: Means nothing to me. When I see a pregnant woman, sex seems a million miles away.

CAROLINE: I'm afraid there were no angels.

STELLA: Can I feel?

STELLA *gets up and puts her hand on* CAROLINE's *stomach.*

STELLA: Amazing. It's always amazing. (*She sits back in her own chair.*) When you think it's completely formed. (*Pause.*) Would you mind if I knit something for it? It could wear something for a week.

CAROLINE: I'd like that. Thanks.

STELLA: How do you feel? About the adoption?

CAROLINE: I don't feel anything. I don't feel a child inside me.

STELLA: No. (*Pause.*) I could take photographs. As you get bigger. You'll be bloody beautiful.

CAROLINE: You're different this morning.

STELLA: I'm wet.

CAROLINE: Yes, but nicely. Does it happen often? Like last night?

STELLA: I suppose so. (*She shrugs.*) I pinched his socks. Look. Mine were sodden. Tell you a lot about him, don't they? (*Visualising.*) Men's bedrooms. Someone should do a study of them. (*Laughs.*) Me, I suppose. (*Shrugs, perhaps only half serious.*) I'm quite terrifying you know. (*She gets out some eye make-up remover from her handbag, dabbing off her mascara.*) With men. It feels like lust, but it's loathing really. Quite cold.

CAROLINE: Why? What's the point?

STELLA: Because of the way they look at you. The way they sniff you about.

CAROLINE: Wow!

STELLA: They do exist, Caroline. It's not my imagination. There's something I do, have done before. If I land a really three-star macho man . . . you know, the whole image . . . never stops telling you what a great time he's going to give you. He's going to make you really cry out, you know, like drowning . . . and all this whispered or licked at you across his MG or yelled in your face on his Yamaha, a great gob full of, whatever, garlic or grease or fag smoke, and fucking Brut – always Brut or Prick or Stud or Come or whatever they can dream up to call that very unpleasant smell that hides that other very unpleasant smell which is the smell of them getting turned on to you – and they want to get it up through your tights in some car park so that they don't have to cope with you afterwards, you know, because they have no feeling, nothing . . . dead eyes, dead bodies. So what I do is this. I give him . . . Mr Godsgift . . . I give him the real Penthouse cliché, right. Lick my lips, touch myself, scream a bit, play scared when he steps out of his knickers, I mean – awestruck – and I get so very excited in the first number. I always try and break things in his bedroom – preferably something expensive – because I'm so wild for it – and I give out all the words. And I can get it done in a few minutes and, well, there he is, slack-jawed, grinning, notching me up on the barrel, three-quarters asleep. So I leave him for a few minutes, then kiss him like it was love – and then I get going on him for round two. Well! Bit of a laugh, bit nervous now, Mr Godsgift, bit sheepish . . . but it's going to be a great story for his pals in the morning: 'You should have seen this slag – she couldn't get enough of it!' And he makes ride number two, sometimes makes ride number three, perhaps, but he's losing and he's worried and he's sore and he's fucking terrified, and the NEXT time I make certain he falls apart. I'm surprised. I'm very disappointed he can't make it. I even get angry with him. And then I get dressed and come home and stand under the shower and scrub him off me and if I could stand boiling water I'd boil myself clean to the marrow.

CAROLINE: That's horrible.

STELLA: There are men doing it every day. It's my little bit to restore the balance. I mean, fuck it. If you're holding someone's hand you've only got one free to grab with.

CAROLINE: What's the point?

STELLA: That's why you're so nice, Caroline. Because you're still interested in finding out. I envy you. I really do.

CAROLINE: Is that why you do this? To harden me up?

STELLA (*angrily*): That's exactly what I mean; the social worker mentality. Poor Stella – there must be a jolly good reason why she's like this.

CAROLINE: I'm sure there is.

STELLA: You must tell me sometime.

CAROLINE: It doesn't matter.

STELLA: No, really, I'm fascinated.

CAROLINE: You and Kate'll get on like a house on fire.

STELLA: Is this your teacher friend?

CAROLINE: Yes.

STELLA: We'll have to compare notes.

CAROLINE: I didn't mean that. Kate has no notes to compare. She's gay.

STELLA: What? And you think I must be?

CAROLINE: No, but you both . . . you both forgive women but you won't forgive men.

STELLA: Oh, come off it. I mean, what does that mean? I forgive women but not men. I can't abide most women.

CAROLINE: It wasn't a criticism.

STELLA: Well, I'm not gay. That's one thing that can be said for Fran – she can't stomach all that Women's Movement crap. At least men laugh.

CAROLINE: So do women.

STELLA: Ach.

CAROLINE: It's true, I've laughed more with you than with any man.

Pause.

STELLA: What do you do? When you're down on the beach?

CAROLINE: Nothing. Walk.

STELLA: Are you going today?

CAROLINE: Probably. (*With an air of self-mockery.*) D'you know why I came back here? Why I go on the beach? I thought it was going to be romantic. To walk by the sea at night, tasting the salt on my tongue. But I don't like the cold! I spend a lot of time in cafés warming up and anyway, after all, being pregnant isn't very spectacular, is it? Just lots of days to fill up.

STELLA: Can I come with you today?

CAROLINE (*surprised*): Yes. (*Delighted.*) Yes!

STELLA: Right, I'll fetch the thermal underwear.

CAROLINE: Actually, what's strange is it never feels so cold if there's two of you.

Scene Five

STELLA *and* CAROLINE *are outside. They're on bicycles, enjoying themselves.*

STELLA: What about Max?

CAROLINE: What?

STELLA: If it's a boy: Max?

CAROLINE: Max what? Maxwell or Maximillian?

STELLA: Max! Max-Max.

CAROLINE: I like that. Does it get into the top three? Is it a one to watch?

STELLA: Well, what's there at the moment? Nathan . . . ugh!

CAROLINE: Joshua . . .

STELLA: Well it's better than those two!

CAROLINE: Max. Yes it's good. Okay – Max if it's a boy.

STELLA: And Stella if it's a girl. Definitely!

CAROLINE: Oh, definitely. And we'll come to visit once a year, and have wonderful times and eat sweets.

STELLA: Right, it's a deal. Wonderful times with Auntie Stella . . . only promise – no bike rides.

CAROLINE: Yes. Bike rides! He/she will be a cycling fanatic. He/she will have black hair possibly, or brownish hair or blonde hair . . . black hair: all me; brownish: me/Robin; blonde: me/John. And will laugh lots, little or not at all . . . that's Robin lots, John little and me not at all. I'll tell you . . . it's crucial what happens now, you know. By the time you're born, it's all decided. This child will love the sea, bicycles and the sound of women talking.

STELLA: And whale music!

CAROLINE: It would be nice, wouldn't it?

STELLA: Yes, it would be nice.

CAROLINE: Come on, slowcoach.

STELLA: Hang on. Caroline, I'm getting off.

CAROLINE: No, don't stop!

STELLA: I'm shattered!

CAROLINE: Oh come on, pathetic. I don't want to get off. It's extraordinary. (*Cycling off.*) I don't want to get off ever . . . ever . . . ever . . . ever . . . ever.

Scene Six

STELLA's *Flat.*
STELLA *is alone.* FRAN *enters.*

FRAN: Hello. I came as soon as I could dump Heidi. Is she upstairs?

STELLA: Yeah. I think she's asleep.

FRAN: What did the doctor say?

STELLA: Nothing much. He said she'd be okay. She's not going to lose it.

FRAN: Thank God for that.

STELLA: He didn't really want to know. He was very polite, but he kept saying 'miss', 'miss', and it stuck in his throat.

FRAN: Perhaps he thought she'd wanted to, that she'd . . . uh . . . done something to herself.

STELLA: Very likely. Anyway, at least she's stopped panicking.

FRAN: So, and what was it, she just started bleeding?

STELLA: Yes, apparently. But she's been down for days. I thought she was just pissed off, I mean, do you know that neither of those blokes write to her . . . she's had a couple of postcards! It's pathetic. It makes me bloody weep when I see the post.

FRAN: What, not even her mum?

STELLA: Oh, she writes, and the schoolteacher friend, but, well I don't know . . .

FRAN: That's what she wanted though, isn't it?

STELLA: She doesn't know what she wants. Nobody sane spends nine months lugging a spare tyre around and then gives it away to some self-righteous couple.

FRAN: They don't have to be self-righteous.

STELLA: Of course they do. You've got to be white, comfortable and self-righteous.

FRAN: So what do you suggest? And actually, Stella, you're wrong, actually, completely. So tell me, what do you suggest she does?

STELLA: OK – she's a really nice girl. She's lovely. It'll be a lovely kid. She ought to be able to keep it.

FRAN: She doesn't want to.

STELLA: How does she know?

FRAN: How do you?

STELLA: I don't, but Christ, Fran, she's got practically no choice, and that can't be right. It makes me go bloody reactionary, you know. I keep getting the urge to drag one of those men up the aisle with her. I know it's ridiculous.

FRAN: Well that's no use. If she's not up to keeping the child herself, marriage won't help. I mean, that's a really daft argument, it's like you get these couples who say they'll only get married if they have children, but that's rubbish because there's got to be something really tough there when a child comes along . . . because it really can destroy things . . . between people . . . that's what happened to me, Stella, isn't it? Because, I mean, you can ignore things – but a child – if there are cracks anywhere it'll force them apart. You can be sure of that . . . I think I'll go up, anyway, see if she's okay, poor old sod.

CAROLINE *appears in the doorway.*

CAROLINE: Speak for yourself.

STELLA: You're supposed to be in bed.

CAROLINE: Yes, nurse.

STELLA: I'm serious.

CAROLINE: In a minute. Hello Fran.

FRAN: Hello love.

CAROLINE: I'm still here. (*Sitting down.*) Despite Mr Maloney and the instruments of torture. What's the matter with you two?

STELLA: There's nothing wrong with me.

FRAN: There's nothing wrong with me either. Except I've left Graeme.

CAROLINE: You're joking.

FRAN: Do I mean left him? Yes, I think I do.

STELLA: Bloody hell!

CAROLINE: When?

FRAN: Sunday. Sunday was not a good day, apparently several football teams had lost the previous afternoon. I was supposed to realize this . . . because that's why no appearance until sometime in the middle of the night. And then of course, Heidi and I are supposed to leave him alone all the next day and not talk, or you know, live much. And certainly expect no help or whatever else a man can contribute to family life. So I had a major wobbly. Oh, there was a classic – you'll love this, Stella – 'Why do you think Mothercare is called Mothercare?' . . . this is a question from my husband . . . 'Think about it' he said . . .

STELLA: I bet you did.

FRAN: I did not. I went to my own mother and she's caring for me!

STELLA: Terrific!

FRAN: Well, it's not permanent, I don't suppose. I'm waiting for signs of repentance. I know how many clean pairs of socks he's got left.

STELLA: How do you feel?

FRAN: All right, but my mum keeps crying. Anyway we'll sort it all out, I expect. Hey! I bought you some avocados! Any use?

CAROLINE: What a memory!

FRAN (*to* STELLA): The way to Caroline's heart . . . the avocado pear.

CAROLINE: This is absolutely true. Can I eat one now?

STELLA: I'll get a spoon.

CAROLINE: Get three spoons!

STELLA *exits.*

FRAN: You okay?

CAROLINE: Yes, I'm okay. He said the baby's still going strong.

FRAN: Stella said. That's good.

STELLA *enters with the spoons.*

STELLA: Three spoons.

CAROLINE: Wonderful. These must have cost you a fortune.

FRAN: They did!

STELLA: Well bloody hell, we're celebrating!

FRAN: Right. I've shown Graeme the yellow card.

CAROLINE: And I'm still pregnant.

The three girls are close and relaxed. They continue to eat happily as the lights fade.

ACT TWO

Scene One

The Seafront. Spring.
    KATE *and* D *are waiting for*
CAROLINE *by a children's amusement
park or playground, suggested by a climbing
frame or slide, or both.* D *is seventeen and
wearing a leather jacket decorated with
political and feminist badges. She has just
been spraying a poster with spray paint and
has some over her hands.*

KATE: Now you've got paint all over your hands.

D: It'll come off.

KATE: Christ, it's freezing. Where is she?

D: I'm not cold. It's great, Kate, really exciting. It's so quiet but it's really noisy as well, isn't it?

KATE: What was so offensive about that poster?

D: It was sexist.

KATE: How? It was for gardening tools.

D: For whose garden?

KATE: How should I know? Just gardens.

D: Well, if it's for anyone's garden, how come you never see a woman in a gardening advert? Like on telly – who shows you how to cultivate the world's fattest potatoes? The man. And then who shows you how to peel them? His missus. That's sexist. My dad doesn't even know where our garden is. He never goes out the back door unless he's sneaking off to the pub.

KATE: I see. And that will be perfectly clear to passers-by, will it?

D: Yes. . . . Probably.

KATE: Mummy, mummy why has that got 'This is a sexist poster' written on it? Because D's Dad never goes in their garden.

D (*sulkily*): You taught me to spray posters.

KATE: Did I?

D: You're sorry you brought me already.

KATE: I didn't bring you – I couldn't get you out of the van.

D: You said I could come.

KATE: Yes, I did, and here we are, getting cold. Happy?

D: You're like you are in class.

KATE: Really?

D: Sarcastic. Unfriendly. It's because you don't want the others to know.

KATE: Fine. There's nothing for them to know.

D: I've told you how I feel. Are we going to sleep together?

There is a pause. KATE *is flustered.*

I know you want to.

KATE: You don't know anything.

D: No Miss, sorry Miss. Can I play on the swings, please Miss?

KATE: Go to hell.

D *sulks.*

Oh, for God's sake. Look, I'm sorry. I can't stand long journeys. I get ratty.

D: It's not that. It's Caroline.

KATE: What about her?

D: You used to teach her too, didn't you?

KATE: So?

D: Whose baby is it?

KATE: Well, it certainly isn't mine.

D: No. (*Triumphantly.*) She's not gay then, is she? (*She slides down the slide or equivalent gymnastic apparatus.*) Wheee!

KATE: You're very naive, D. Apart from anything else, being lesbian doesn't stop you having children.

D: Must make it hard work though. But she's not, anyway, is she?

KATE: Ask her yourself.

D: Why did she come down here?

KATE: She was born here. It's her home.

D: She should have got rid of it. I would have. The guy just gets on with his life. Why can't she get on with hers? It's typical.

KATE: Well, it's also inescapable. You

can change most things, you can't redistribute wombs.

D: The day will come.

KATE: I hope not.

D: She could've still got rid of it.

KATE: She didn't want to.

D: What, just so as to give it away? Stupid.

KATE: Don't act thirty. You're a very bright seventeen, you're a dim thirty.

D: My English teacher told me that when someone pulls rank on you in an argument it normally means they're losing.

KATE: I never said any such thing.

D: Anyway I'd hate to be thirty. I don't care if I'm dead before then.

KATE: You will.

D: I'm not talking about you. I'm talking about me. About my generation. Things are moving really quickly, really fast. Seven-year-olds are on the pill or they're winning Nobel prizes. Everything's speeded up. It's to do with technology. There's no room for age now. So you've got to get everything done, cram it in quick. I think soon everyone will die before they're twenty-one.

KATE: Fine – we'll have to warn Caroline she's only got a day left. Who's been telling you all this nonsense?

D: Actually, it's not nonsense. Lots of people know about it. It's got to happen because there's nothing left, there's not enough energy to go round anymore. (*She climbs to the top of the slide or frame.*) I can see Caroline. (*She waves.*) She's seen us.

KATE: Where? (*Scanning the landscape.*) She thinks she's Sylvia Plath, you know. That's why she wanders around here. She's living it all out.

D: Is she?

KATE: Look at her. She's inside some poem – you know? – and it's very sad.

D: She doesn't look sad to me. She looks bloody enormous.

KATE: Where are the things for her? Have you got the bag?

D: You left them in the van.

KATE: Oh, right.

CAROLINE *enters, heavily pregnant.*

Where've you been?

CAROLINE: Walking. Hello.

CAROLINE *and* KATE *kiss.*

Hello D.

D: I hid in the luggage.

D *looks to* KATE *for support, but does not get any.*

CAROLINE: Fine. I hope you don't mind the floor.

D: No. I can sleep anywhere.

CAROLINE (*smiling*): How was the journey?

D
KATE (*together*): All right. A pain.

CAROLINE: You must be tired.

KATE: I'm frozen.

CAROLINE: You met Stella?

KATE: We said hello. How are you?

CAROLINE: Fine. Did I tell you? I've been seeing a lot of Fran?

KATE: Yes, you did.

CAROLINE: She's fine.

KATE: Are we going back?

CAROLINE: Sorry, you're cold.

KATE: Is there any food?

CAROLINE: Oh, I don't know. Probably.

KATE: We haven't eaten. I wanted to get here in daylight.

CAROLINE: Sorry, I'm not thinking. I should have made something.

KATE: We'll get a takeaway.

CAROLINE (*to D*): How's D?

D (*simply*): Great. It's a great place.

CAROLINE (*gently*): What've you got on your hands?

KATE (*laughing*): She's been defacing posters.

CAROLINE: Ah.

KATE: You can tell her about it on the

way. Along with your catastrophe theory.

D: No. You two go on. I'll catch up.

KATE: What are you doing?

D: Just going for a short walk. You two have a nice chat.

D *exits*.

CAROLINE: What does that mean?

KATE: Search me. Oh, come on, I'm not going to run after her.

CAROLINE: Poor Kate.

KATE (*looking after* D): Poor Kate. (*Looking at* CAROLINE.) So . . . you look OK.

CAROLINE: I am OK.

KATE: I've missed you.

CAROLINE: Despite D? I've missed you too.

KATE: Oh yeah! I know what you miss . . . someone to wash your knickers . . . food.

CAROLINE: Don't start.

KATE: Did you get the cheque?

CAROLINE: I will pay you back.

KATE: I don't want it back.

CAROLINE: Then don't play the martyr.

KATE: Speak for yourself.

CAROLINE: Have you seen him?

KATE: Which him?

CAROLINE: John.

KATE: Yes.

CAROLINE: And?

KATE: I've seen him. Look, neither of them want to know, Caroline.

CAROLINE: How do you know? (*She moves away.*)

KATE: You shouldn't have gone through with this. It's absurd.

CAROLINE: It moves. It kicks. I can feel it.

KATE: Yes. And you'll feel it afterwards too. It's conscience. And you can't have that adopted.

CAROLINE: But I could have killed it. Is that what you're saying?

KATE: No, that's not what I'm saying. (*Pause. Then angrily.*) Does it make it easier, Caroline? To use those words? To justify yourself? In which case, OK. Yes. You could have killed it. Or you could keep it. But neither of those is romantic, is it?

CAROLINE *is hurt. Stung. She moves away towards the water.* KATE *exhales sharply, frustratedly.*

(*Shouting after* CAROLINE.) Is this what you're going to live off . . . all the pain you've stored up over the winter?

CAROLINE: I'm happy, Kate. I could stay here for ever.

KATE: Well, I'm cold, and I've got the van, and I'm driving back. Coming?

CAROLINE *turns. A beat. She smiles.* KATE *smiles.* CAROLINE *returns. They embrace.*

Scene Two

STELLA's *Flat.*
FRAN *and* D *are sitting together.*
STELLA *has wet hair and is drying it with a hair dryer.* KATE *is apart from them, waiting for* CAROLINE *who is supposedly outside, making a telephone call to her mother.*

FRAN: Are you keen on motorbikes, then?

D: No, I just like leather jackets.

FRAN: Oh, I see . . . I love the badges. Is that the fashion now?

D: I don't know anything about fashion. Fashion stinks.

STELLA: Why?

D: Well, for a start . . . shaving your armpits or your legs or something . . . or painting your bloody face up. It's all rubbish.

STELLA: You won't mind if I dry my hair?

FRAN: Long phone call.

STELLA *turns off the drier.*

STELLA: What?

FRAN: No. I was just saying to Kate – Caroline's been gone a long time.

STELLA: Oh?

KATE: I don't know why her mother couldn't have come down. You'd think she might have made the effort.

FRAN: Well, it's quite a way, isn't it?

KATE: So's Leeds. They don't want to see her, do they? Then Caroline can turn up in April with a flat stomach and they can all pretend it never happened.

STELLA: They might be in for a shock. I don't think she'll give it away.

FRAN: Nor do I.

KATE: Nothing to be smug about, really, is it? Who's going to look after this baby?

FRAN: Lots of girls manage.

KATE: Caroline can't manage herself.

STELLA: How do you know?

KATE: I live with her. I make her bed.

STELLA (*acidly*): She makes her own bed here. Perhaps she thinks you like doing it.

KATE: You see, I don't think knitting matinée jackets is caring, particularly. I think that's easy. It's like buying a child a pet.

STELLA: No one's encouraging her to do anything.

KATE: No? Oh, Christ, D, do you have to pick your nails!

D: Great party. Who died?

FRAN: You're right, D. It's Caroline's birthday. It won't be much of a party at this rate.

STELLA: It won't be much of a party anyway. Without any men.

KATE: Well, that's a start.

FRAN (*cheerfully*): We'll have to play some games.

STELLA: We'll have to get some drinks in.

D: Why?

STELLA: Why what?

D: Why do we have to get drunk, or play games?

KATE: What do you suggest then?

There is a pause.

D: I'll go to the off-licence.

KATE: No . . . I'll go. I've got the van.

D *makes as if to go with her but* KATE *turns at the door pointedly.*

See you in a minute.

Scene Three

The Promenade. Night. The sound of gulls is heard.
    CAROLINE *is alone.* KATE *enters, looking for her.*

KATE: Where've you been?

CAROLINE: Ringing my mother.

KATE: For an hour? Oh Caroline.

CAROLINE: I don't feel much like parties.

KATE: No. Me neither. Let's go somewhere . . . in the van.

CAROLINE: Where's there to go?

KATE: Well, we don't have to GO anywhere. We could just get in the back and have our own party. I bought this in case. (*She produces a bottle of Martini.*)

CAROLINE: No thanks, Kate.

KATE: Why not?

CAROLINE: I don't want to.

KATE: Why not?

CAROLINE: And I rang John.

KATE: And what did John have to say?

CAROLINE: He played Happy Birthday on his mouth-organ.

KATE: Was that instead of a card?

CAROLINE: Oh, probably, Kate. But he's sweet.

There is a pause.

D'you know what? I keep finding myself talking to my stomach. Extraordinary. But it's really nice because it's not like . . . it's not the same as talking to yourself, is it?

KATE: No, it's not the same. I want to kiss you for your birthday.

CAROLINE *kisses* KATE *quickly on the cheek.*

CAROLINE: Thanks . . . I think we'd better go back now.

Black-out.

Scene Four

STELLA's *Flat.*
CAROLINE *is standing in the middle of the room. A game of charades is in progress and* CAROLINE *is holding up four fingers.* STELLA, KATE, FRAN *and* D *are sitting around.*

STELLA: Four words.

KATE: What is it? Book, film or play?

CAROLINE *shakes her head.*

It's got to be.

FRAN (*who has chosen the charade*): Or a well-known phrase or saying.

KATE: Typical. OK, four words.

CAROLINE *shows her third finger, and makes the 'small word' sign.*

STELLA: Third word, small. An? At?

KATE: In? With?

D: To?

STELLA: On? Of? Off?

CAROLINE *nods furiously.*

KATE: Of?

CAROLINE *shakes her head.*

On!

CAROLINE *points at* D.

STELLA: To! Something something to something.

CAROLINE *nods, raises her fourth finger and points to herself.*

KATE: Fourth word. You?

CAROLINE *encourages her.*

You? Run?

CAROLINE *indicates 'no'.*

STELLA: Girl?

D: Woman? Baby? Mother?

There are 'looks' all round.

CAROLINE: No.

STELLA: Not you. Uh . . . body? No. Uh . . . Caroline?

CAROLINE *nods, encouraging, and does the 'whole phrase' sign.*

KATE: Whole something. Something – Caroline? Not Caroline?

CAROLINE *shakes her head. Makes 'second word' sign.*

KATE: OK. Second word.

CAROLINE *shows 'two syllables' sign.*

Two syllables . . . first syllable . . .

CAROLINE *points to her stomach.*

D: Tum? Stomach? Belly? Stupid?

CAROLINE *nods, lies down on the floor, enacts a thirty second labour, pulls out an imaginary child, slaps its bottom. 'It' cries.*

KATE: Baby.

CAROLINE *nods. There is silence.*

FRAN: Oh come on, it's obvious.

KATE: Something . . . not baby . . . to . . . you, Caroline, something.

FRAN: No! Do the first word, Caroline.

CAROLINE *is upset but tries hard to look happy.*

STELLA: Pleased. Smiling. Joy. Happy!

CAROLINE *nods.*

STELLA: Happy! Happy nearly baby to? Where does baby come into it?

KATE: Birthday! Happy Birthday to . . .

CAROLINE: Me.

A pause. Everyone is strained.

FRAN: Right! Happy birthday to you. . . . Come on, (*singing.*) 'Happy Birthday' . . .

The others join in the singing.

CAROLINE: Thanks. (*At a loss.*) Uh, whose turn is it?

Scene Five

STELLA's *Flat. Night.*
KATE *and* D *are sleeping together in a narrow single bed.* CAROLINE *enters but seeing the situation starts to leave.*

CAROLINE: Oh.

KATE (*half voice*): I'm awake Caroline. Caroline. I'm not asleep.

CAROLINE: We'll wake D up.

KATE: No, we won't. Put the light on.

CAROLINE *switches a lamp on.*

What are you doing?

CAROLINE: I couldn't sleep.

KATE: What's the matter?

CAROLINE: Can't get comfortable.

KATE: The baby?

CAROLINE: It's taking me over. There's no room in the bed for me. Now it's got hiccups. I'm not joking.

KATE: What time is it?

CAROLINE: I don't know. Late. Early. (*She looks at* D.) She's remarkable.

KATE: What? Not waking up? She doesn't sleep at night, she dies.

CAROLINE: You're much closer, aren't you?

KATE: It's a very small bed.

CAROLINE: You know what I mean. Since I left.

KATE: What do you want me to say? Look . . . I started off teaching her English, now I'm teaching her this.

CAROLINE: God, you're patronizing.

KATE: I don't think so. I'm trying to get with it. Otherwise I get hurt when lessons finish . . . you know?

CAROLINE: It's your own doing, Kate.

KATE: I'm sure it is. Well you know us gays . . . We like getting hurt. Oh, and corrupting minors, let's not forget that . . .

CAROLINE (*cheerfully*): Oh, shut up.

KATE: Why does Stella put out that sleeping bag for us? Was she embarrassed?

CAROLINE: I don't know.

KATE: Do you talk to her?

CAROLINE: Of course I talk to her. What do you mean?

KATE: No, I mean TALK to her. Confide in her.

CAROLINE: I suppose so. A little. Yes.

KATE: Because you won't with me, will you?

There is a pause.

CAROLINE: I haven't seen you, Kate. I'm getting used to you being around again. And anyway there's D.

KATE: So . . . (*she looks at* D.) What's happening then? What are you going to do?

CAROLINE: I don't know. Have the baby.

KATE: And then?

CAROLINE: And then? I don't know.

KATE: Are you coming back to my house? Well what?

CAROLINE *does not respond.*

You can't stay here.

CAROLINE: Probably not, no.

KATE: What have you been doing? What do you do with your days?

CAROLINE: Walk. Think.

KATE: Have you thought about me much?

CAROLINE: Oh, Kate. I have written to you.

KATE: I've thought about you, Caroline. All the time. I've been sleeping in your bed at home . . . We could bring the child up together. I've thought about that, too. I've got enough money. We could manage.

CAROLINE: No.

KATE: I'd love her – I'd love both of you. I could look after you both, please.

CAROLINE: I don't want to.

KATE: The house is empty without you. Haven't you missed it? Haven't you missed Leeds at all?

CAROLINE: Look, this is impossible. Yes, I've missed Leeds. For God's sake, Kate, you're in bed with D, you've got someone. I haven't missed you, Kate, if that's what you're asking me . . . I mean, of course I have, but not in the way you want. I just don't have those feelings for you. I never have had.

KATE: Never?

CAROLINE: I'm pregnant – look! – a man did this, and I miss HIM desperately.

KATE: Oh, so you *do* know who the father is?

CAROLINE: I know who I'd like it to be. There was never anything between me and Robin. I was flattered. That he would be prepared to leave someone for me. I wasn't attracted to him. I was attracted to that.

KATE: But you had sex with him.

CAROLINE: The world doesn't stop.

KATE: I wouldn't know.

CAROLINE: No.

KATE (*bitterly*): Still, we'll be able to tell by the colour of its hair, won't we?

CAROLINE: That's the point. That's why I can't talk to you. Because you don't want to hear really, do you?

KATE: Not about you with men. No, not particularly. Why is that the point?

CAROLINE: Because we can never discuss the fact that I wanted a man, Kate. Can we? And I did. Not furtively. Not cluttered. Not ashamed of it. Not . . . it was like an ache . . . it was an ache. Sounds like dogs, doesn't it? But it was so good with John and me. Grabbing each other all the time. Just grabbing. And then we started to trade that in for a whole lot of crap like the future and what it meant and what we, and I . . . because you see all these people, these couples, and they can tell you about their relationship and what it means and you can see this energy totally strangled. They sit facing each other over tables when they really want to be grabbing, under the tables, grabbing. I'm not talking about orgies, I'm talking about honesty between people. And I'm angry because we had that and then we swapped it. So you see, Kate, it's hopeless, isn't it? I mean, look at us. D's dreaming and you're dreaming and I'm dreaming and it's hopeless. I

end up with Happy Birthday played down the telephone. (*Pause.*) I'm sorry, but sometime you had to hear that.

There is a long pause.

KATE: Yes, I did need to hear that Caroline. But why now? Why not a month ago? A year ago? (*She pauses.*) You've always reeled me in a bit, haven't you? A look, a word, just enough to keep me there, hanging, foolish. Well, thanks. Thanks a lot.

CAROLINE: I'm going to bed now. Goodnight.

KATE: Goodnight, Caroline.

CAROLINE (*touching* KATE): You're my dear friend, Kate, and your letters have kept me going. Sleep tightly.

KATE: You too.

CAROLINE *goes out, turning off the light.*
A beat.

D: Kate?

KATE: Yes?

D: I wasn't asleep.

Scene Six

The Beach. Late Afternoon.
Everyone – CAROLINE, STELLA, KATE, D, FRAN – is in a very loony mood. It is the late afternoon of a silly, wonderful day. They are all wearing cowboy hats and flowers and a picnic hamper is in evidence. There is a lot of fooling about and screaming. FRAN has a plastic bundle – a kite.

CAROLINE: People were looking at us.

FRAN: I don't care.

STELLA: I do. I've got my image to think of. I'm not supposed to have fun in public.

FRAN: Shut up.

STELLA: And as for you Kate, you are an embarrassment.

KATE: This is true.

STELLA: Roll your trousers down.

KATE: Absolutely not.

STELLA: In that case I'll roll mine up!

FRAN: Now I'll have to roll mine up. C'mon Caroline.

CAROLINE: Must I?

D: Yeh. Go on Caroline.

CAROLINE: Okay. How do I look?

STELLA: Ludicrous.

KATE: Wonderful.

STELLA: Wonderful *and* ludicrous.

KATE: Are we going to hop?

STELLA: No!

FRAN: Yes!

STELLA: This is false pretences. You said picnic. You said fun day on the beach. You said as one with nature. You did not mention hopping.

KATE: Hop!

STELLA *hops.*

D: Yeah!

KATE: That is an impressive hop Stella. That is a hop you have kept under a bushel.

FRAN: What about my hop? C'mon! Give me marks out of ten!

KATE: Okay sisters. Stop hopping. Hop not and assess. We're looking for bounce, we're looking for style and we're looking for stamina . . .

FRAN: Hurry up.

KATE: Stella?

STELLA: Well . . .

FRAN: Hurry up! I'm knackered. (*She keeps hopping.*)

STELLA: It *is* difficult.

KATE: Caroline?

CAROLINE: Great, Fran.

FRAN: Great is not a mark! Are we talking 8? Are we talking 9?

KATE: What are we talking girlies?

D: Foot down!

FRAN: No!

STELLA: Definitely!

KATE: I'm sorry Fran. That was a foot down.

STELLA (*tragic*): Shame.

FRAN: I'm sitting down. I may sulk.

CAROLINE: You're all crazy.

FRAN: Come on love. Sit down.

CAROLINE: I think I'll lie down.

KATE: Oh no. Out of the way! Clear the runway!

D: Yeah! The kite.

KATE: Come on. Shift your bums. We're having a test drive. Out of the way weedies or I'll kick sand in your face!

FRAN: School bully.

KATE: The very same. Okay! Here we go!

She runs away from the group. The kite remains earthbound. Great applause.

STELLA: Rubbish!

KATE: It's off the ground! It's off . . . It's . . . There can't be any wind.

STELLA: You're joking. (*It's windy.*)

FRAN: I think we're struggling on the skill front here.

KATE: You'll eat your words, shitbags. I give up. I'm dying. Argh! Minister to me. Gorge my fat carcass with cake, you hussies!

STELLA: We come, your majesty!

STELLA and FRAN attack KATE and stuff cake in her mouth.

KATE: Get off! Argh! Help! Help! Gay-bashers!

D (*to CAROLINE*): How are you feeling?

CAROLINE: Fine. Exhausted. My stomach hurts from laughing. (*Looking at the cavorting.*) Watch out, Fran, she bites!

KATE: Yes, I do!

D: It's been a really silly day.

CAROLINE: Yes, lovely.

KATE *and* STELLA *are now tickling* FRAN *who makes groaning, hysterical noises.*

STELLA: It's a whale! (*She accompanies* FRAN *with whale music.*)

D (*to CAROLINE*): I'll be back in a minute. I'm going to find some shells.

KATE: Where are you going, D?

D: I'm going hunting for shells and things. Maybe have a paddle.

KATE: We're just going to eat. What's the matter?

D: Nothing. (*Truthfully.*) I'm happy. You coming?

KATE: Yeah. Sure. I'm stupid. A paddle! God! If I die, Fran, you can have my back copies of *Spare Rib*.

FRAN: Well hurry up – I'm ravenous.

D (*picking up the kite*): And I'm going to get this bloody thing to fly if it kills me.

KATE: Don't you dare scoff all the doughnuts.

KATE *and* D *exit.*

STELLA: Who wants some coffee?

FRAN: Please.

CAROLINE: Not me. Ugh, this yoghurt's leaking! It's all over the sandwiches.

STELLA: What flavour?

CAROLINE: Uh . . . muesli.

STELLA: Oh, that's all right then.

FRAN (*examining her damaged flower*): My flower's not very well.

STELLA: Actually, they're really nice, aren't they?

FRAN: What?

STELLA: Those two lunatics.

CAROLINE: Yes, they are.

FRAN: Kate's really different . . . you know . . . from school. Funny, isn't it? Like you expect, well I've always sort of thought that if you're . . . you know, if you don't like men, that you'd be –

STELLA: What are you wittering on about?

FRAN: Well, they're just nice, aren't they?

STELLA (*laughing*): That's really deep, Fran.

FRAN: You know what I mean. We've had a lovely day, haven't we?

STELLA *starts off singing 'Didn't we have a lovely time, the day we went to the seaside'.* FRAN *chimes in with whale music.*

CAROLINE (*a bit pale, piqued, lying down but speaking happily*): I'm so tired! I'm going to close my eyes and when I wake up I want it to be morning and we can start today all over again.

FRAN *and* STELLA *tuck into the picnic.*

FRAN: Do you know – I've never won anything before.

STELLA: Me neither.

CAROLINE: You won Space Invaders.

STELLA: This is true. Was I brilliant?

CAROLINE: Devastating.

FRAN: I didn't hit anything. I don't like the noise it makes when you do. (*To* CAROLINE, *indicating a coat.*) Do you want this over you, love?

CAROLINE: Please.

STELLA: How are things with Graeme?

FRAN: Oh, okay. He's taken Heidi to his sister's today. (*She bites into a doughnut.*) Yes, all right, it'll never be marvellous. Um . . . this is obscene. The thing is I can't talk to him. He has made an effort . . . sort of . . . you know, after I went back, but we can't have fun . . . not like this. I never laugh. I haven't laughed like this since I was at school. Sad, isn't it?

STELLA: Yeah.

FRAN: For him too. Half the time he doesn't know why he infuriates me. Neither do I really.

STELLA: But you think it will last?

FRAN: I don't know. I know him. I'm not dim, I know what he's like . . . you know – other women and things. But then you see at the end of the day he's still my husband. He's still Heidi's dad. Does that make any sense?

STELLA: Yes . . . Hey! They've got it up, look!

FRAN: Yeah!

STELLA: Look at Kate! She's an absolute maniac. They're getting soaked!

FRAN (*to* CAROLINE): Do you want something to eat?

CAROLINE: Oh, no thanks . . . my stomach hurts. I've been laughing too much.

STELLA: You'd better take it easy you nut. We don't want you going into bloody labour on the beach.

KATE *rushes on, kicking her wet legs at the others.*

STELLA: Get off!

KATE: We got it working! Good, eh? I'm freezing! Ach, give me a doughnut before I die. Is there any coffee left? Look at D. She's like a little kid. (*Yelling.*) Come in number fourteen – your time is up! (*Shaking her head.*) Mad as a hatter. You asleep, Caroline?

CAROLINE: Hardly.

KATE: Oh I'm so bloody wet! What am I doing? (*Lying down beside* CAROLINE.) Well that's it. I've had it. God!

D *comes on, looking mischievous, with a bucket and a spade.*

D: Mummy, mummy – I've found a contraceptive on the beach.

KATE: What's a beach?

FRAN: O God . . . she really has! Don't be bloody revolting . . . let's have a look.

D *displays the bucket.*

STELLA: Ugh, I can't stand those things. Look at it. Christ!

FRAN: It's a drowned semen.

STELLA: I thought it was supposed to be impossible underwater.

D: I've decided – it's a message in a bottle.

STELLA: She's absolutely right. Can't read it though – it's in French!

KATE: Don't show it to me, you perverts, it's probably poisonous.

D *teases* KATE *with the bucket.*

KATE: Go away! Ugh, how gross! Girls . . . this bag has been raped.

FRAN: No, no, of course! It's a silly fish!

There is general laughter.

STELLA: Silly fish! Well, that's it . . . can you imagine . . . next time you're in Boots: 'Excuse me, I'd like a packet of three silly fish, please!'

FRAN: I don't know how it happened, Doctor, we HAVE been using silly fish.

KATE: O throw it away, D. It makes me feel sick.

CAROLINE (*urgently*): Fran . . . I think something's happening. O God, Fran, what's happening?

KATE: Caroline! What's the matter?

STELLA: Caroline?

CAROLINE: Oh, my God.

FRAN: We'd better get the van, Kate. Stella – you ring the hospital. Tell them we're coming in. (*To* CAROLINE.) You're going to be all right, lovely. Just relax. Come on . . . remember your breathing.

CAROLINE: What?

FRAN: I think you're probably going to have your baby, love. Don't worry, it's all going to be fine.

Scene Seven

A hospital side room. There is a right angle of connected grey plastic seats. One table, with a pile of magazines on it. FRAN, STELLA, KATE and D are there. It is late. D is asleep with her jacket over her.

FRAN: Now I know what men feel like.

There is a pause.

STELLA: Why do hospitals always smell the same?

There is a pause.
KATE *puts down a magazine, gets up and walks about.*

KATE: This is ridiculous. What's going on?

FRAN: She'll be a while yet, I expect.

KATE: I think they should have let one of us stay with her.

FRAN: Oh come on. They've been ever so good. We might have been downstairs with the dads.

KATE: You're joking.

STELLA: Look at D.

KATE: Will it be all right? I mean why is it so early?

FRAN: It's not that bad. A few weeks. She should be okay. They've got babies in here two months premature – perfect. It's ever such a good hospital.

KATE: I didn't like that doctor.

FRAN: He didn't like you.

KATE: Well, they're so bloody clinical. She didn't know what was going on. They should have let one of us stay with her. I mean, there's no bloody father on the scene. If there had have been they would have had him in holding a leg or whatever it is they do. I could have done that.

FRAN: He did explain, Kate. If her mum comes in time then she'll be with her and if not then one of us can go in.

KATE: Why one? Why not all of us?

STELLA: Christ, Kate, forget it will you? There's no point. Fran's right. Things could have been a lot worse. At least they treated her like a human being. They don't always.

FRAN: What do you mean?

STELLA: Well (a) she's not married, and (b) she's giving the kid away. She's not normal, is she? I don't mean the nurses. It's the other women. They can be so bloody cruel. I've seen it. The way they say Miss. Miss.

FRAN: Oh I don't know. I don't think that's fair.

STELLA: Well . . . perhaps things have changed.

KATE: Since when?

STELLA: Since a long time ago. (*She gets up.*) Doesn't that smell get to you? That certainly hasn't changed. It's ten years since I went inside a hospital. I was pregnant. (*Very quietly.*) Before I came down here. One fuck! I was actually in love with the bloke . . . he's married now . . . really nice guy . . .

KATE: And what – did you have an abortion?

STELLA: No, I didn't, I was going to have the baby, that was the idea. (*Pause.*) But anyway, I started to lose it. I didn't really know, but I was at home, not actually at home, round my uncle's – in the kitchen – and I was really pathetically naïve. And I was sitting in this chair, and feeling lousy, and not knowing what to do about it or what, you know, how to say anything – because, I mean, obviously my uncle didn't know what was going on. So I just sat there, and I knew I was in this pool of blood, and I just waited until he left the room, whatever he was doing, can't remember, and then just got up and rang the hospital. I mean I can't remember all the details, but they said it was hopeless, and my mother was there for a bit, and then I was in this bed, and I'd been knitting a little jacket for it, and the Nurse had come round to give me a wash, and she came back and said I shouldn't bother with knitting, but I thought bugger that, and then you know, literally minutes later, I'd sort of passed it into the bedpan. I felt like a little girl. And they got a priest and he did a kind of baptism and he gave it a name. I mean I didn't, I hadn't thought of names or anything and he said best to call it Frances, because it was impossible to say, you know, if it was a girl or a boy, so I did. Well I just said okay Frances is fine. Anyway, anyway, why am I telling you all this? . . . Oh yeah, . . . the smell, that's what reminded me. And the other women . . . smug with their rings on their fingers and their stupid husbands.

FRAN: That's where the matinée jacket came from for Caroline, isn't it?

STELLA: Yeah, I thought I might as well finish it off.

FRAN: You kept the wool.

STELLA: Oh me – I'm a right hoarder.

KATE: Is it upsetting you? Being here? I could run you home, love.

STELLA: No, don't be daft. It's all water under the bridge. Besides, got to see it through: a bit of the old solidarity.

KATE: That's it. A bit of the old solidarity.

The NURSE *enters.*

NURSE: You've got company. (*Off.*) Here we are. Shall I get you a cup of coffee?

SHEELAGH O'BRIEN, CAROLINE's *mother, enters. She is drawn, anxious.*

SHEELAGH: Thank you. Uh, no thanks. No coffee thank you.

NURSE: Okay. Right, I'll leave you to it.

SHEELAGH: Thanks. Hello Kate. Hello Fran.

FRAN: Hello. Uh, Stella, this is Caroline's mother. This is Stella.

KATE: And this is D. Wake up love.

SHEELAGH: Oh no, don't worry . . .

D: What? I was asleep.

KATE: This is Caroline's mother.

There are hellos all round. SHEELAGH *replies with 'pleased to meet you'.*

SHEELAGH: Caroline's told me how kind you've been.

KATE (*sharply*): Have you seen her?

SHEELAGH: They let me look in. Just for a second.

KATE: Did they.

SHEELAGH: She wasn't really aware of what was happening, I don't think. They've given her some Pethadin.

FRAN (*disappointed*): Oh why?

SHEELAGH: I don't know. I should think they know what's best though, don't you? They've got one of those monitor machines on her that measures the contractions . . . and one for the baby's heartbeat. Anyway, the doctor told me they're very happy with her . . . Do you mind if I sit down? It's quite a drive.

KATE (*sharply*): Are you not going back in then?

SHEELAGH: Uh, yes. I said I'd come and give you a weather report. Yes. I just thought I'd . . .

SHEELAGH *gives the impression that she is near breaking point. The girls generate an atmosphere that veers between sympathy and hostility.*

You've all been so good to Caroline. We're very grateful.

FRAN: Is Mr O'Brien not with you?

SHEELAGH: No, he, uh, well, he's not as well as he might be. He gets very agitated, you know, if there's any stress. I don't think he'd be much help just now. No, but you must all be exhausted. Have you not been home or anything?

FRAN (*after a beat*): We've just been saying . . . it must be quite a novelty here to have a pile of women pacing up and down outside the delivery room.

SHEELAGH: Yes, that's right. (*Compulsively putting her hand to her face.*) Goodness, I think I must be more tired than I thought. Oh, I've got some chocolate. Would anybody like some?

FRAN: No, thank you.

STELLA: Not for me, thanks.

SHEELAGH: Are you sure? Go on, do have some please.

STELLA: Oh all right then.

SHEELAGH: Fran?

FRAN: Okay. Thanks.

SHEELAGH: Pass it round. Do.

KATE: Thanks.

They munch the chocolate in silence. The atmosphere is very strained now.

SHEELAGH: You must understand – I shall be fifty soon, and Caroline's my only child, and my husband's too, and then you see, you only want what's best, don't you? What's for the best . . .

FRAN: You don't have to explain to us, Mrs O'Brien.

SHEELAGH: No – but I don't want you to think that we don't love her, because we do, we do love her. She's our daughter.

There is no response.

She asked us not to come down, you know . . . Did she tell you that? *Several* times. But it's the same, as I said to my husband – when all's said and done . . . it's our grandchild, isn't it?

KATE: Well, don't try and persuade her to keep the baby . . . not because of your guilt . . . not when she's so vulnerable. She's already wasted getting on for a year. Don't ask her to waste the rest of her life.

SHEELAGH: And is that what you think families are? A waste?

KATE. I'm not talking about families. I'm talking about a single girl with a course to finish and no help, no father. It's not fair . . . on Caroline or the child.

FRAN: Kate . . .

KATE: Well, I'm angry. I'm bloody angry. You couldn't even teach Caroline to look after herself and then you talk about families.

SHEELAGH: And what have you taught her? She lives in your house. Don't you feel responsible?

KATE (*the irony not lost on her*): Oh, Christ . . . (*She sighs.*) Yes, I do, actually. I do feel pretty bad about it.

STELLA: I'm sorry. I don't see the point of all this.

FRAN: Neither do I. Blame . . . what does it matter? It won't change anything. That baby up there in the delivery room – Caroline's baby – somewhere around there's a couple, a woman who's been waiting for this moment. And it's going to make them so happy. I wish people would stop talking like the whole thing was a tragedy. No-one's died.

KATE *goes over to* SHEELAGH *and touches her.*

KATE: I'm sorry. You start thinking of people only by their title: woman; mother; teacher . . . I'm always shouting off about that, but I do it myself all the time.

D: I've got a headache. Anyone got an aspirin?

STELLA: Sorry.

FRAN: No, sorry love.

KATE: We're in a hospital, and no one's got an aspirin.

SHEELAGH: Hang on, I should have some in my bag . . . somewhere . . . (*She fishes out a box of mints.*) I stopped at one of those service places on the way down, and I bought these for Caroline . . . she doesn't like mints.

FRAN: Well I do.

STELLA (*smiling*): You're a bloody dustbin, Fran.

FRAN (*smiling*): Yeah.

The NURSE *comes in.*

NURSE: Would you like to come back in, Mrs O'Brien? The head's appeared. It won't be long now.

Scene Eight

The hospital ward. CAROLINE *is in bed, surrounded by flowers. Her mother is visiting her.*

SHEELAGH: I'd better go. Kate's waiting to come in.

CAROLINE: Yes.

SHEELAGH: Did I tell you? I spoke to Daddy. He thought we might try and go on holiday together.

CAROLINE: He hates holidays.

SHEELAGH: He wants to do something for you.

CAROLINE: Yes.

SHEELAGH: Well, you don't have to say yet.

CAROLINE: Right. You'd better get off. It's a long drive.

SHEELAGH: It's not too bad. I surprised myself, you know, coming down. Perhaps I'll feel less nervous now about the roads to Leeds.

CAROLINE *nods.*

I wish I could stay.

CAROLINE: There's nothing for you to do. I'm fine. Fran and Stella will supervise.

SHEELAGH: I used to think Fran was such a scatty girl . . .

CAROLINE: Oh no.

SHEELAGH: Oh, I realize now. Anyway, I'll go . . . (*She sighs.*) . . . you know before I come in I keep thinking of all the things I want to say . . .

CAROLINE: There's no need, Mum.

SHEELAGH: I think there is, darling . . . (*Abruptly.*) So – can I tell Daddy you'll think about where you'd like to go.

CAROLINE: Did you see him, Mum?

SHEELAGH: Daddy?

CAROLINE: My baby. Did you?

SHEELAGH: Yes.

CAROLINE: I wanted you to.

SHEELAGH: Caroline – it's not too late if –

CAROLINE: Don't . . .

The NURSE *bustles by.*

Nurse, Nurse, how's my baby?

NURSE (*in a hurry*): Fine.

CAROLINE: Because Sister mentioned he was a bit grizzly last night.

NURSE: No, he's fine. He's bonny. All right?

CAROLINE: Yes. Thanks. I just wondered.

The NURSE *is going.*

(*Stopping her.*) Nurse, yesterday they brought him up to me . . . you know, in the, it's not the incubator, uh . . .

NURSE: Baby trolley.

CAROLINE: Yes, the baby trolley. I just wondered whether I could, you could, whether I could see him this afternoon?

NURSE: I expect that'll be all right. I'll ask Staff. OK?

CAROLINE: Thanks. Sorry to . . .

SHEELAGH (*to the* NURSE): Thanks. (*To* CAROLINE.) That'll be nice.

CAROLINE: Yes.

SHEELAGH: Everybody seems very nice. You mustn't worry about him crying. It's perfectly natural.

CAROLINE: I know.

SHEELAGH: You cried all the time. Your lip always stuck out. (*She demonstrates.*) Your father used to say he could sit on it. Shall I send Kate in?

CAROLINE: Please.

SHEELAGH: I was thinking. It's a shame neither of your friends turned up.

CAROLINE: Which friends?

SHEELAGH: I'm afraid I don't know their names . . . uh. (*She thinks, cannot remember and gives a short laugh, shaking her head.*) The boys from Leeds.

CAROLINE (*nodding*): Oh yes. It's a shame. Whatever happens . . . we'll talk, eh?

SHEELAGH (*nodding*): Yes, that's right. Bye bye, darling.

CAROLINE: Bye, Mum.

SHEELAGH (*very quietly*): Bye.

SHEELAGH *exits.*
KATE *enters.*

KATE: Hello.

A buzzer sounds.

Goodbye!

CAROLINE: I'm sorry. There's no time.

KATE: Well, I'll see you next week, won't I?

CAROLINE: I'm only going to stop a day or two, Kate. I think I ought to go home for a while.

KATE: Right . . . I rang John.

CAROLINE: Yes. These came. (*She indicates some flowers.*)

KATE: He said he'd come down – if I thought it would help.

CAROLINE: It wouldn't.

KATE: That's what I said.

CAROLINE (*wryly*): Say it with flowers! Where's D?

KATE: In the van. She says goodbye.

CAROLINE: Well, I'll see her in Leeds won't I?

KATE: I expect so.

CAROLINE: Right. I'm glad you came. I'm glad you were here, Katie.

KATE: So am I.

CAROLINE: Have I been a fool? Is that what you think? (*Pause.*) I have, haven't I?

KATE: I don't know, sugar. Whatever you do, you lose. Whatever you'd done. Whatever you'd done, there's loss. It's a bugger, isn't it?

CAROLINE: Yeah.

KATE: Well hurry up and get out. You'll get soft in that bed.

CAROLINE: My milk's come through, Kate.

KATE *sighs. A pause. They embrace.*

KATE: Every day something will happen, won't it? Today it's your milk, then there'll be birthdays and reminders and . . . for ages . . . you'll have to get tough, won't you?

They just sit there on the bed, embracing. CAROLINE *starts beating* KATE *on the back.*

What are you doing?

CAROLINE: Getting tough.

KATE: You! (*She gets up, smiling.*) See, you, shitbag.

CAROLINE: Yeah. See you.

STAFF (*off*): Come along, fathers. Out, out, out. The buzzer's gone.

KATE *exits.*
The STAFF NURSE *enters.*

STAFF: Nurse says you'd like to see baby.

CAROLINE: Please, if that's OK?

STAFF: Well you can, but I'm afraid it can only be for a few minutes because I know that uh, Doctor Minareau and Mrs Holden have arranged for his new, for the adoptive parents to meet him today.

CAROLINE: Ah.

STAFF: I think you knew that, Caroline, didn't you?

CAROLINE: I don't know. Yes, probably, you lose track of what day it is. Oh, never mind then.

STAFF: I said you can see him for a few minutes now, and then later on if you want.

CAROLINE: Lovely. Thanks. That would be lovely.

STAFF: So, I'll get nurse to bring him up. Now, are you still leaking a bit or is the injection taking care of it? (*She means* CAROLINE's *milk.*)

CAROLINE: It's all right I think.

STAFF: Good.

STAFF NURSE *exits.*

STAFF (*off*): Mrs Fitzgerald, there's no need to walk like that. Goodness me! It's a baby you've had not an elephant.

MRS FITZGERALD (*off*): It felt like an elephant.

STAFF (*off*): I'm going to tell that nice husband of yours you're being an old misery guts.

We watch CAROLINE *in bed for as long as the moment can be held whilst she faces the reality of losing her baby.*
The NURSE *pops her head round.*

NURSE: Caroline, I'm sorry but they're already here.

CAROLINE: Never mind. What a bore.

NURSE: Look, I'll make sure he's brought up to you as soon as we can. Sorry. (*Pause.*) Have you got enough books?

CAROLINE: Oh yes.

NURSE: It's good isn't it? So many of your friends come to see you. We were just saying. Really nice.

CAROLINE: Right.

NURSE (*at the door*): Shout if . . .

CAROLINE: Do they seem nice? His new mum and dad?

NURSE: I don't know Caroline. I haven't met them.

CAROLINE: But they looked nice, did they?

NURSE: Uh, yes. Of course.

CAROLINE: Can't I ask that? I'm not allowed to ask if they look nice?

NURSE: I honestly have hardly seen them, but yes they seemed very nice.

CAROLINE: I just wish people would stop treating me as if I were a martian. You know?

NURSE: Uh.

CAROLINE: Forget it. Really just forget it. Could you draw the curtains please? I'm tired. I think I'd like to sleep.

The NURSE *draws the curtains and the room goes dark.*

Scene Nine

The Seafront.
FRAN, STELLA *and* CAROLINE (*with* HEIDI *in her pram*). STELLA *is carrying* CAROLINE's *haversack.*

FRAN (*referring to* HEIDI): Look at her face! And this was clean on this morning. I don't know, madam.

STELLA (*laughing*): She's great.

FRAN: When she's asleep. (*To* HEIDI): Hey, how could you manage to get choc-ice up your nose?

STELLA: Easy, isn't it Heidi?

FRAN: And she's finished it, little sod, I'm starving! (*To* HEIDI.) Hey, I'm starving.

STELLA: Christ, Fran, you should be enormous.

FRAN: I am. I've just got a tight skin.

STELLA: Twit.

FRAN: Yeah. Holds it all in. (*To* CAROLINE.) All right love?

CAROLINE: Yes. I'm just having a good breathe. Souvenir.

FRAN: Oh, don't say that.

STELLA: Hey no drama, right? If you're going to get weepy, either of you, you can piss off.

FRAN: Hark at tough tits.

STELLA: Too right. When she goes I'm going to have to get a job.

CAROLINE: I haven't gone yet.

STELLA: Well, you're not staying with me. It's Spring. I'm getting out my butterfly outfit.

CAROLINE: Wow the tourists.

STELLA: The idea is to frighten them off. (*Referring to* CAROLINE's *haversack.*) What's in this Caroline? Bricks? You're never going to manage it yourself. Is Kate going to meet you?

CAROLINE: Yes. Oh, listen, Fran I've left all the things, the clothes, and the books and things. Stella's got them.

FRAN: Lovely.

STELLA: And the Whale Music.

CAROLINE: Uh, no. I kept that. I mean, I'd like to keep that if that's OK?

FRAN: Sure.

A woman, VERONICA, *walks by with a very young baby in a pram.*

VERONICA (*to* FRAN): Hello, how are you?

FRAN (*uncomfortable*): OK. Just dashing.

VERONICA (*to* HEIDI): Isn't she a beauty? Hello fishface.

FRAN: She's a monster. You can have her. (*She wants to keep going.*)

VERONICA: You're joking. (*Indicating her pram.*) Yes, I'll do a swop. This one . . . no one told him about sleep.

FRAN: Ha! Listen, I'll give you a call . . . or pop in or something?

VERONICA: Smashing.

CAROLINE *goes up to* VERONICA's *pram.*

CAROLINE: How old is he?

VERONICA: He's new. He'll be three weeks tomorrow.

CAROLINE: What do you call him?

VERONICA: What do we call him? Oh . . . rat . . . pig. His name is Josh.

STELLA: Caroline. The boat.

CAROLINE: Right.

VERONICA (*to* FRAN): Bye now. Pop in.

FRAN: I will. Bye.

They walk on.

I'm sorry. I couldn't ignore her.

CAROLINE: Doesn't matter. Really. (*To* STELLA.) Josh!

STELLA: Urgh!

CAROLINE (*sighing*): Oh.

They walk on.

STELLA: So, when shall we three meet again?

FRAN: Four.

STELLA: What? Oh, yes, four.

They reach the boat.

CAROLINE: You must come up to Leeds.

STELLA: Yeah.

CAROLINE: Fat chance.

STELLA: I'll surprise you. Look, I'm going

now. I'm a lousy waver. (*She walks away.*)

FRAN: You'd better get on love.

CAROLINE: Yes. I'd better . . . look, I'll . . . uh . . . you know.

FRAN: I know.

CAROLINE: I want to say sorry, but I'm not sure what for.

FRAN: Then don't.

STELLA (*walking back*): Right. Push off, I'll see you in Leeds.

CAROLINE (*she looks at them both*): Hey . . .

STELLA: What?

CAROLINE (*thinking; shrugging*): Just hey. (*She starts to go, then turns.*) See you.

FRAN: Yeah.

CAROLINE *exits.*
   The lights fade as STELLA *and* FRAN *watch her go.*

THE END

A LITTLE LIKE DROWNING

For my mother and her mother
Fra il mare giallo e le dune
Cesare Pavese

A Little Like Drowning was first performed by the CV-One Theatre Company in March 1982 at the start of a national tour. The cast was as follows:

NONNA MARE
LEONORA MARE *Nonna as a younger woman*   Jenny Howe
ALFREDO MARE   Haluk Bilginer
JULIET JARRETT   Rosalind March
GIOIA   Peta Masters
THERESA   Rosalind March
PETER   Haluk Bilginer
ANASTASIA   Peta Masters
GIANNA   Rosalind March
GRAEME
FATHER DAVID
BRUNO
EDUARDO   Bob Hewis

Directed by   Bob Lewis
Designed by   Bernard Culshaw
                  and Vickie Le Saché
Lighting by   Peter Gilbert

The play is set in England, Ireland and Italy between 1920 and the present.

N.B. The writing allows for some doubling not least in the case of LEONORA and NONNA, PETER and ALFREDO.

ACT ONE

Scene One

The present. England.
OLD LEONORA (*known as* NONNA)
*is in a rocking chair. There is a Giuseppe
Di Stefano record playing. LEONORA is
seventy two. ANASTASIA is a small girl,
LEONORA's granddaughter.
ANASTASIA struggles in with pitcher,
bowl and towel.*

NONNA: Thank you darling. (*NONNA
kicks off her sandals, ANASTASIA
pours water into the bowl, and she plunges
her feet in, sighing. ALFREDO appears
as for the wedding night, 1926, with an
identical toilet, same jug and bowl and
takes off his shirt – not in the light – and
begins washing, humming the Giuseppe
Di Stefano. NONNA and ANASTASIA
do not see ALFREDO.*

NONNA (*to* ANASTASIA): I love this
music. Don't you love it?

ANASTASIA (*shrugs*): It's all right. No:
not really. I don't understand it.

NONNA: It's a crime that none of you
speak Italian. Will you cut my toenails
for me this evening, Anastasia?

ANASTASIA: OK.

NONNA: My feet are so ugly aren't they,
and my legs, hands, everything. Look
at my hands and look at yours . . .

ANASTASIA: I'll get the scissors.

NONNA: Thank you darling. (*Sharp.*)
Where is your sister? What are they
doing?

ANASTASIA: Don't know. They're in
the other room, I expect.

NONNA: Is that boy still here?

ANASTASIA: Expect so.

NONNA: Puttanas! Licking each other's
backsides. Tell her it's time they packed
up, she sent her – (*Makes a distasteful
sound.*) – tell her to come in here!
Wouldn't be any of this if your parents
were in. Can't even get them to make
me a cup of tea.

ANASTASIA: OK.

*She exits. NONNA pours on more water.
Remembers.*

Scene Two

*The past. Italy, 1926.
The wedding night.* LEONORA-
ALFREDO. *Candlelight.* LEONORA
brushing out her hair. ALFREDO *takes
off his shirt. Wears trousers with the braces
dangling.* LEONORA *wears a white cotton
nightdress. She is 16.*

ALFREDO: Think I'm drunk.

*He comes up behind her, puts a hand
to her breast.* LEONORA *flinches.*

ALFREDO (*admonishing her*): Hey! Hey!
We're married, remember?

LEONORA: I'm just getting ready to come
to bed, Alfredo.

ALFREDO: And I was just trying to
help.

Pause. He watches her.

ALFREDO (*proudly*): Signora Mare.

NONNA: Signor Mare.

ALFREDO (*Great sentimentality. Kisses
her fingers. Sucks on the wedding finger
down to the ring*): With this ring I thee
wed. With my body I thee worship.

LEONORA (*holding on to his hand*): With
this ring I thee wed. With my body I
thee worship.

ALFREDO: Is that what we actually
said?

LEONORA: Yes, of course.

ALFREDO: Didn't understand it
properly. I still don't see why we couldn't
have been married in England.

LEONORA: This is our village.

ALFREDO: Our village! I've never lived
here.

LEONORA: Your family. Your family's
village.

ALFREDO: Half the time I didn't
understand what anybody was saying.
They talk so bloody quickly. Too much
time in England I suppose. My Italian's
rotten.

LEONORA: You should let me
translate.

ALFREDO (*defensive*): I can understand
most of it. Just takes me time to speak
it, that's all. I'll be all right in a day or

two. It's not good Italian they speak here.
Your Italian. Terrible dialect.

*He goes to a bottle of wine and pours
himself a drink.*

LEONORA: Siamo paesani. That's what
you married. You know that.

ALFREDO: I wasn't criticising you.
You're not real paesan. You're brighter
than anybody in this place.

LEONORA: I don't think so.

ALFREDO: You want some wine?

LEONORA: No thank you. Oh yes. From
your glass.

She drinks from his glass.

ALFREDO: I love it when you talk like
that.

LEONORA: Like what?

ALFREDO: You're like a little girl.

LEONORA: I am a girl. (*Looks up at him.
Simply.*) I'm a bit nervous.

ALFREDO: Have some more wine.

LEONORA: No. It makes me queasy.

ALFREDO: Don't worry. (*Pause.*) Stuffy
in here, isn't it? Terrible.

LEONORA: I don't mind.

ALFREDO: I hate this country. If you
close the windows you can't breathe and
if you open them you get bitten to
death.

LEONORA: It's your cologne. The
mosquitos like it!

ALFREDO: It's got nothing to do with
my cologne.

LEONORA: I remember when you came
here for a holiday. I was twelve.
(*Mischievously.*) Yes, because you were
thirteen and fat! and I saw you walking
up past the olives to this house. Your
brother was with you and you were
wearing a sailor's outfit. White with
stripes. I wanted you to notice me but
you didn't. Not that there was anything
to see. I went home and said a whole
rosary that one day you would marry
me.

ALFREDO: Is that true?

LEONORA: Yes, it's true.

ALFREDO: So you had God organising

this, did you? Or was it the Madonna?

LEONORA: Alfredo, don't!

ALFREDO (*smiles, pleased with himself*):
I remember that suit. To think you
thought about me all that time ago, and
I didn't know you existed and were
growing up in Valvori – sleeping and
waking and growing up to become my
wife. I'm glad you said your rosary.

LEONORA: Are you really?

ALFREDO: Yes . . . and you see God
gave you those eyes and that hair so I'd
notice you. And those breasts. Shall we
go to bed now?

LEONORA: Yes.

They blow out the candles.

*

*Morning. Warm shafts of light through
the shutter. The eiderdown stripped off
the bed.* ALFREDO, *braces and
trousers, with bowl and jug, preparing
to shave.* LEONORA *kneels, her head
on the sheet.*

ALFREDO (*defensive*): Ma che fai?

Silence. He washes.

ALFREDO: Look. I hope you're not going
to judge me on last night. I was drunk.
It's no use crying.

Silence. He lathers his face.

ALFREDO: Besides. You seemed, well,
oddly-shaped. Maybe not. We'll have
to get used to each other, that's all. Put
it down to experience shall we? Andiamo
eh! Now, stop crying and come here and
kiss your husband good morning. It's
beautiful. Warm. Marvellous.

*He goes to the windows. Opens the
shutters. Strong light on them both.*
ALFREDO *looks down.*

ALFREDO: Funny. What are those people
doing? Why are all those people down
there? Your mother! Your family!
What's going on?

LEONORA (*not looking up*): We must
show them the sheet.

ALFREDO: What!

LEONORA: We must show them the sheet
from our bed. With blood.

ALFREDO: They can piss off!

LEONORA: No! They want to see that I was pure. It was the same for my mother. And your mother.

ALFREDO: Well, how can we?

LEONORA: Wait.

She gets up and takes the water jug and spills a little of the water on to the sheet.

LEONORA: Give me your razor.

ALFREDO *hands her his razor. He snatches it back.*

ALFREDO: No!

He looks at her then quickly slices across his finger. He pulls the sheet off the bed and stains the damp patch with his blood. Then, together, he and LEONORA step out onto the balcony and hold the stained sheet aloft like a flag. There is a cheer from below. ALFREDO looks at LEONORA. They smile foolishly.

ALFREDO (*quietly to* LEONORA): Thank you.

Applause.

ALFREDO (*proudly*): Thank you! Thank you!

They kiss. More applause.

Scene Three

The present. England.

GIANNA *comes in. She is around seventeen.*

GIANNA: What is it, Gran?

NONNA: What are you doing?

GIANNA: Nothing much. Talking. Having coffee.

NONNA: You make yourselves coffee. What about my tea?

GIANNA: Can't Stacey make it? Graeme's got to go soon.

NONNA: Ach Graeme! I want you to come in here please. Tell him to do up his trousers and come in here.

GIANNA: O Gran, really! Why do you talk like that? It's horrible.

NONNA: Is it? So are abortions.

GIANNA: O Christ.

NONNA: That's right.

GIANNA: Honestly Gran, I don't know what you think we're doing when the door's open and Stacey's barging in every five minutes.

NONNA: Oh yes . . . little innocent.

ANASTASIA *comes back with scissors.*

GIANNA: Gran thinks we're having group sex in the dining-room.

NONNA: If you're not doing anything wrong then it won't hurt to sit here, will it?

GIANNA: Oh come on, we're not children . . . it's so embarassing to have to sit here with you and Stacey.

ANASTASIA: Thanks.

GIANNA: You know what I mean. You don't like it when, I don't know, Chris comes round, do you, and you have to play in here?

ANASTASIA: Don't mind.

GIANNA (*sarcastic*): Course not.

ANASTASIA: I don't.

GIANNA: Tch. Well, can we at least listen to some decent music? This stuff's out of the ark. (*to* LEONORA.) And please don't start taking your corsets off in front of everyone.

NONNA: Oh goodness! Don't think you're so high and mighty, madam. I've seen you do a wee-wee on this carpet.

ANASTASIA *giggles.*

GIANNA: Well, how nice for you. I mean I suppose I must have been nearly two. Sorry to be so weak-bladdered.

NONNA: Well I'm over seventy-two. Sorry to be so old.

GIANNA: It's much better, Gran, when you have your room and we have ours. Then we can all do and say what we want without rubbing each other up the wrong way.

NONNA: I thought that was what you were doing . . . rubbing each other up the wrong way!

NONNA *and* ANASTASIA *laugh.*

GIANNA: You've got such a dirty mind!

NONNA: When you've had your mind as long as I've had mine, yours will be dirty too. And I'll tell you something else for nothing. Experience! You can't take that to the launderette. It doesn't wash out. It's like always drinking from the same cup – coffee, tea, soup, wine – in the end everything tastes the same. And bitter.

GIANNA: I have absolutely no idea what you're talking about.

NONNA (*bitter*): No – of course not.

GRAEME (*from the doorway*): What's going on? You coming back in or what?

GIANNA: We've been summoned. Sorry.

GRAEME: I don't mind. I'm really into opera. Who is it?

GIANNA (*sardonic*): Terrific!

GRAEME: Evening Mrs M.

NONNA (*to* GIANNA *of* GRAEME): Why don't you make him a cup of tea?

GRAEME: I'm fine thanks. Just had some coffee.

NONNA: I'd like a cup of tea.

GIANNA: Stacey's not doing anything.

ANASTASIA: Nor are you. I've got homework to do.

GIANNA: Well, I've got A levels to do!

GRAEME (*chiding gently*): Have you? This year?

GIANNA: Next year. And she gets away without serving in the café.

GRAEME: Oh come on. She's only a kid.

GIANNA: So were we only kids and we had to do it.

NONNA: Poor you.

GIANNA: Yes, poor me!

GRAEME: You could still make your Gran a cup of tea. You should be good at it.

GIANNA: Don't you start! Don't be taken in by her, (*Referring to* ANASTASIA.) I have to pick up her smelly knickers and her smelly bloody socks and iron her smelly gymslips and . . .

ANASTASIA (*cutting in*): Mum irons my gymslips, actually!

GIANNA: Oh! That's all right then, if Mum does it.

ANASTASIA (*sulkily*): Yeah.

GRAEME: Gianna!

GIANNA (*to* GRAEME *as she exits*): You could at least offer to come with me . . .

GRAEME: In a minute. This is really nice. (*Referring to the music.*)

NONNA: The other side's beautiful. Puccini.

GRAEME (*nodding inanely*): Italian. Really nice.

NONNA: You're a bit fat (*Laughs.*) Do you like macaroni?

GRAEME (*taken aback*): Uh . . .

NONNA: Why doesn't Gianna bring you to supper? I make lovely gnocchi.

ANASTASIA: He's not fat. (*to* GRAEME.) You're not.

GRAEME: I don't mind.

NONNA: I'll tell you something – when I was Gianna's age, I was thin, terrible thin! Had to cut my wedding ring in half – really! – and join it back together. My fingers were so thin. And then babies . . . (*sighs.*) Had to have the ring sawn off my finger and the bits put back, baby by baby, bit by bit, until the original size. See? (*Shows ring finger.*)

ANASTASIA: That photograph of you in the hall – the coloured-in one. You're really pretty in that.

GRAEME: What photograph's this?

ANASTASIA: Come on, I'll show you. (*To* LEONORA.) Can I show him the wedding photograph too? From your bedroom? (*Going out.*)

GRAEME: When was that?

NONNA: 1926. In Italy. Valvori.

GRAEME: I bet it was an incredibly long exposure. (*To* NONNA:) Can you remember how long you had to keep still? I bet the photographer counted – oh twenty. Can you remember?

NONNA: No.

GRAEME: Pity. (*Going out.*)

ANASTASIA: Graeme!

GRAEME: Excuse me.

Alone NONNA *takes a swig from a sherry bottle, and then settling herself into a relaxed position, falls asleep. The music continues.* GIANNA *comes in with tea tray. Sees* NONNA *asleep.*

GIANNA (*cheerfully*): Typical.

She sits down and drinks the tea herself. GRAEME *comes back in.*

GRAEME: Hi.

GIANNA (*referring to* NONNA): So much for the tea.

GRAEME: We've just been looking at those old photographs of her. Everybody in your family looks exactly the same. There's one with your Gran and Grandad dancing and he's all in black, little white tie, straight out of the Godfather.

GIANNA: Tell her. She'll love that.

GRAEME: And I really fancy her in it. Dead sexy.

GIANNA: Is she? What? More than me?

GRAEME: Dunno. Can't remember. Let's see now.

He starts kissing her. ANASTASIA *enters.*

ANASTASIA: Yuk!

GIANNA *pushing* GRAEME *off.*

ANASTASIA: She's got a cold, you know.

GIANNA: I love you too.

ANASTASIA (*giggling*): Gran's showing her drawers again.

GIANNA: Well at least she's wearing some. (*Laughs.*) Honestly, she's an absolute liability. Was she smoking do you know? You've got to watch for that. She's always practically setting herself on fire. It's a miracle she doesn't – the amount of alcohol she consumes – really! – she's a highly inflammable lady. (*Laughs.*) I'd better cover her up.

ANASTASIA: I'll do it.

GIANNA: The thing is, Stacey, if you think you're being good it doesn't count.

ANASTASIA: It does! (*Goes over to the sleeping* LEONORA.)

GIANNA: Fine. (*To* GRAEME.) She thinks doing that will get her two weeks off purgatory.

ANASTASIA: It might! I got grandfather ten years off yesterday. With one decade of the rosary. It's in my missal.

GIANNA (*shaking her head. To* GRAEME): The Catholic Church! Actually, while you're at it you'd better wake her up. She'll be annoyed if she misses her tea.

ANASTASIA: OK. (ANASTASIA *is looking to prove she's mischievous. She takes a jug of water and holds it over* NONNA's *head.*) Shall I?

GIANNA: Stacey!

ANASTASIA *dips her finger into the jug and flicks water at the sleeping* NONNA *who wakes with a start. Her shawl slips from her shoulder. She's furious.* ANASTASIA *giggles stupidly.*

NONNA: Eh Aiee! Anastasia! Bitch! You come here! I'll bash you! Bagasce!

GIANNA: Stacey, say sorry, you idiot!

NONNA: Get her! I'm wet! Catch her!

ANASTASIA *still giggling, embarrassed, runs out of the room.*

NONNA: I'm wet. Cow. Bitch.

GIANNA: It's OK Gran. She was just showing off. It wasn't much. A few drops. Come on, I'll dry you off.

NONNA (*tearful*): My scarf's wet. Why did she do that? I was asleep.

GIANNA: She was just showing off in front of Graeme. Here's your tea. Relax.

GRAEME: Shall I go and tell her off or something?

GIANNA (*sharp*): No, you should go home. It's late.

NONNA *starts wiping her face with the red scarf, muttering to herself.*

GRAEME (*offended*): And what's that supposed to mean? God! (*Sighs.*) Night then Mrs M.

GIANNA: Drink your tea, Gran, it'll get cold.

They exit.
   NONNA *ties the scarf around her head.*

Scene Four

The past. England, 1929. Outside the Mare house.
   ALFREDO *leads* LEONORA, *pregnant, down the steps. She is blindfolded with a bright handkerchief.*

LEONORA: Can I look?

ALFREDO: Not yet.

LEONORA: We're outside! Why have you brought me outside?

ALFREDO: Don't be so impatient.

LEONORA: The baby. Alfredo!

ALFREDO: Don't worry. I've got you. I won't let you fall.

LEONORA: Not this baby stupid. Theresa. What if she wakes up and we're both outside?

ALFREDO: A minute. She'll be all right. Anyway, shut up, we're here. Now, I'm going to take off your blindfold but don't open your eyes until I say. (*Does so.*) Right. Now, ready?

LEONORA: Yes. Can I open my eyes?

ALFREDO: Yes!

She does so.

LEONORA: It's dark. It's night. What am I supposed to be looking at?

ALFREDO: This!

LEONORA: What's this?

ALFREDO: The car, mamma! The car!

LEONORA: What car? This car?

ALFREDO (*waving his arms in a flapping gesture of impatience*): Aiee! Which car, which car! Questa macchina qui! Questa stupenda favolosa Alfa Romeo! Which car!

LEONORA: Ah that car! The one you drove home in. And?

She pinches his cheek, teasingly.

ALFREDO: How did you know?

LEONORA: I told you. I saw you drive home in it.

ALFREDO: How did you know to look?

LEONORA: Because you were late. Because I stood in the window waiting for you to come. Because I miss you.

ALFREDO: Okay.

LEONORA: Because you're always late home these days.

ALFREDO: Okay, okay. You can smell the leather, Leonora. So soft.

LEONORA: It's a beautiful car.

ALFREDO (*grunts irritated*): I knew you would be like this.

LEONORA: Like what?

ALFREDO: Criticising me. You can never let me enjoy anything. I work and I struggle. And I mean why do you think I'm late home?

LEONORA: I don't know. Remind me.

ALFREDO: And what does that mean I'd like to know?

LEONORA: It means good you've got a new car.

ALFREDO: We've! We've!

LEONORA: Yes – we've got a new car. And I'm pleased we can afford it because I'm sure I don't know where the money came from to pay for it. Anyway, yes, good, fine. I have to go in now. Your daughter's crying.

ALFREDO: I can't hear anything.

LEONORA: No. You never can.

She turns to go back in.

ALFREDO: Aiee. Leonora. Leonora!

She comes back.

LEONORA: What?

ALFREDO: Mamma. Let's go for a ride, huh? Scusi, eh? Come on. We can put Theresa in the carry cradle.

LEONORA: It's too late. It's too dark.

ALFREDO: Come on.

LEONORA: It's too cold.

ALFREDO: This car has heating. It's an oven with the heater on.

LEONORA: Then it'll be too hot.

ALFREDO: Da mi pazienza!

LEONORA (*relenting*): Okay. (*Laughs suddenly.*) Hey, your face!

ALFREDO (*sulkily*): What's wrong with my face?

LEONORA (*putting her finger to his mouth*): I'll sit the baby on your lip.

ALFREDO: It's important for me to have a good car. Who's impressed – in this country – gl'inglesi – who's impressed with a man comes to do business with you driving a jalopy? Now I'm a serious proposition.

LEONORA: OK, Mr Serious Proposition, take us for a ride and don't spare the horses.

ALFREDO: OK, wife.

LEONORA: OK, husband.

She turns to go back in.

ALFREDO: I'll take you up on the hill and show you the city at night. Eh Leonora, che meraviglia! Hundreds of tiny lights, each one a house.

LEONORA: Oh no. We want to go to the seaside. And don't say it's too dark –

ALFREDO: But that's miles.

LEONORA: And this car can't go for miles or what? I want to walk on a beach with you. Like when we were courting.

ALFREDO: Right. We'll go to the beach. What the hell!

LEONORA: I'll get Theresa.

ALFREDO: And get a coat! For me, too. We'll freeze to death. (*Shakes his head, then looks admiringly at the car. Walks its length proudly, breathing in the smell of paint and leather.*)

LEONORA *puts on a coat or shawl or both.* ALFREDO *puts on a trenchcoat.*

*

The Beach. They walk for a bit, arms round each other, LEONORA *pulls them to one side suddenly, mischievously.*

ALFREDO: Eh! What are you doing?

LEONORA: I want to get my dress wet again! Do you remember?

ALFREDO: I remember. Lunatic!

LEONORA: I remember standing – this is afterwards – standing in your bedroom,

in your dressing-gown – pinned up to the throat, ha!, with you pressing my dress, getting the creases out, that terrible old iron, and you telling me to stop howling.

ALFREDO: Which you didn't.

LEONORA: Imagine you ironing now!

ALFREDO: It had flowers along the bottom.

LEONORA: Yes.

ALFREDO: Tiny embroidered flowers. Lovely.

LEONORA: How do you remember that?

ALFREDO: Kissing the hem of your dress. I remember that vividly.

LEONORA: Getting home late thinking my mother would notice.

ALFREDO: Why? Nothing had happened.

He tries to kiss her legs as he holds the hem of her dress. She, embarrassed, shrugs him off. He looks distressed, hurt. A familiar rebuff.
She moves away. She stands, looking out to sea, she's happy. Unaware of his frustration.

LEONORA (*delighted*): I want to come here every night! The air! It's beautiful. The sea! I feel alive. As if someone slapped my face. Suddenly awake. (ALFREDO's *quiet.*) Hey Alfredo. Fredo!

ALFREDO: Si, si vengo. (*He goes to her, puts his feet under hers and walks along the shore daring the waves.*) Attenzione! Attenzione! (*This is a happy sing-song voice. But the moment passes and they are left silent.*)

ALFREDO: My ears are cold.

LEONORA: I'll kiss them. (*She does so.*)

ALFREDO: Mmm. That's nice. But they're still cold.

LEONORA: I'll rub them. (*She does so.*)

ALFREDO (*distant suddenly*): Listen, what about Theresa?

LEONORA: Oh, she's fast asleep. She'll be fine in your new car. It's so warm! Anyway come on I want to play!

ALFREDO: Now what? Play what?

LEONORA: Hopscotch!

ALFREDO: Madonna! It's dark . . . Leonora . . . How can we play hopscotch?

LEONORA: Easy. Anyway. You can cheat and I won't know. Wonderful. Here's a stone. That's yours.

ALFREDO: Aiee! I don't want to.

LEONORA: Because you don't know the rules.

ALFREDO: Because I don't know the rules.

LEONORA: I'll teach you.

ALFREDO: You're crazy.

LEONORA: Yes.

ALFREDO: And your stomach?

LEONORA: My stomach's fine. We'll have a gymnast.

She marks out a hopscotch pitch.

ALFREDO: I want him to be a singer. Or a footballer.

LEONORA: Him!

ALFREDO: OK. Or her.

LEONORA: I'll start. Watch me!

She throws a pebble.

Scene Five

The present. England. The beach. NONNA is about to throw her hopscotch marker.

ANASTASIA: No! Me first!

She starts to play. They laugh. She makes good progress until she hits the wrong square.

NONNA: No! Wrong square!

ANASTASIA: OK. Now you.

NONNA: I used to be terrific at this!

She can't hop.

NONNA: Oh.

ANASTASIA: Go on.

NONNA: No. I put my foot down.

ANASTASIA: Have another go.

NONNA: I can't. Hopeless. No matter. I'll watch. Where did you get to?

ANASTASIA: Here. Right.

She carries on. NONNA *watches for a while.*

NONNA (*during this,* ANASTASIA *plays, exclaiming, laughing, commenting, etc.*): Do you know something? It makes me laugh. The nicer the day the more you want to go in the water and the farther you have to walk to get to it! And when the weather's bad . . . it's just the opposite. Makes me laugh, I can't swim anyway. I just like the water. The feel of it. Up around my legs. I think I must have been a fish in another life. There are people who believe you have lots of lives to get better in. Lots of chances. I don't think that's against God. What do you think?

ANASTASIA: What? Hang on. Yes! (*She completes the circuit.*) I did it! Did you see? I did it!

NONNA: Yes, darling. Well done. Anastasia, walk out there to the water will you? I want to see how far it is.

ANASTASIA *runs off.*

NONNA: No don't run! I want to see how long it takes to walk there. (*Hums, then loud.*) Anastasia! Anastasia! That's enough. It's too far for me. (*Normal voice as* ANASTASIA *comes running back.*) I couldn't walk all that way. Not on these old legs. Much too far. In a few days the tide'll be nearer and then I'll get in properly. But not today.

ANASTASIA *is back with her. She picks up her bags.* NONNA *touches her cheek.*

NONNA: You're just like your grandfather, Alfredo. That expression. Soft. Both of you gullible. Much too gullible. Shall I tell you something? You mustn't trust everybody. That's what he did. That's what I've done. Gullible. So, don't you forget these things your old Nonna tells you. (*She sighs.*) Mmm, the water in these little pools is so warm. Look! You can see your face in it. (ANASTASIA *looks.*) Sometimes I think I can see other people's faces. Sometimes I stare and stare until they come.

Scene Six

The past. England, 1930.
ALFREDO *and* JULIA JARRETT.
Outside a concert hall. JULIA *impatiently pacing,* ALFREDO *arrives looking sheepish and shifty.*

JULIA: Christ, Alfredo! You're impossible!

She moves towards him.

ALFREDO (*backing off, turning away, and trying hard to look as if he were waiting for someone else*): Uh, don't. I think I saw someone I know. (*Continuing to look away.*) Sorry. Hello. I love you. Don't acknowledge me please.

JULIA: Christ!

ALFREDO: Please don't, Julia.

JULIA: Don't what? I'm not doing anything.

ALFREDO: No. Use that word. I hate the way you use it.

JULIA (*sighing*): Oh.

ALFREDO: Sorry. (*Dismissing himself.*) I know.

JULIA: Can we go in please?

ALFREDO: Right.

JULIA: I mean, the overture will have started.

ALFREDO (*looking about him*): Right.

JULIA: Alfredo, I really can't manage this, you know.

ALFREDO: No, of course, just that I'm convinced I knew him. Friend of my father's.

JULIA: It's a big hall. There's bound to be someone you know. (*Pause, then archly:*) Shall we go in separately?

ALFREDO: Yes. Perhaps that's best.

JULIA: I was joking. No, OK. Right I'm going in. Enjoy the concert – you know – in case we don't get to talk.

ALFREDO (*still not looking at her*): Right. See you in there. Thanks. I love you.

JULIA: You could always wear glasses and a false nose.

ALFREDO: Sorry?

JULIA: You could always wear glasses and a false nose.

ALFREDO (*feels dim, muttering*): Non mi prendi un giro!

*

JULIA *works her way along a packed row in the theatre and sits down. She removes her coat and glances at a programme. It's for a Verdi or Puccini opera. A big moody duet is in full flight.*
ALFREDO *performs the same operation before sitting next to* JULIA *without acknowledging her in any way. After a few bars staring steadfastly to the front, he edges his hand under* JULIA's *skirt and between her legs.*
JULIA *stares ahead as if focussing on the music. After a few bars she sighs and her hand works its way under the overcoat folded on* ALFREDO's *lap.*
They stare ahead. ALFREDO *hums a line of music.*
JULIA *and* ALFREDO *leave as they arrive and stand outside the door which becomes the entrance to a lavatory.*

JULIA (*nervously, giggling*): I can't!

ALFREDO (*impatient, giggling*): Come on. Why not?

JULIA: What if somebody comes? I can't.

ALFREDO: Come on, Julia. Before the interval.

JULIA: Can't we just talk?

ALFREDO: We can't talk here. It's so difficult – you know – if we are seen together . . .

JULIA: Okay, well let's go in there and talk.

She gestures to WC.

ALFREDO: OK. (*Trying to get her in.*)

JULIA: Oh yes! I know your talk.

ALFREDO: Well, and so? I want you. Is that bad? That I want you the whole time?

JULIA (*smiling, shaking her head*): It's wonderful.

ALFREDO (*smiles*): It's fantastic.

JULIA: Come on then. We're completely mad.

ALFREDO: I know.

JULIA: I've never done this before.

ALFREDO: Right. (*Thinks.*) Is that true? (JULIA *nods.*) If you had, Julia, I couldn't. Not if you'd done it before.

JULIA (*touches his lip*): You great baby. (*Laughs.*) Come on!

They go in and close the door behind them.
> *Verdi. Buzz of conversation.*
> *Man paces outside the WC with a cigarette.* ALFREDO *suddenly comes out, obviously trying initially to pretend he's been alone, sees the waiting man and moves into plan B.*

ALFREDO (*briskly*): I'm a doctor. Excuse me. There's a woman in here who's had an asthma attack. I'm going to take her to my surgery.

Then JULIA *appears as* ALFREDO *turns back in. She sees him and the man and moves into plan C as the man moves forward with* ALFREDO, *trying to help.*

JULIA (*briskly*): Ah. It's uh quite all right. Thank you. My husband is going to take me to the hospital.

ALFREDO *and* JULIA *move past the man, arm in arm.* ALFREDO *whispers to* JULIA *who begins to laugh hysterically.*

JULIA (*over her shoulder to the bewildered man*): No, actually my husband is a doctor himself.

Scene Seven

The present. England. Beach.
> NONNA *comes in with her bags,* ANASTASIA *behind her.* NONNA *sits down to take off her shoes.* ANASTASIA *scampers off.*

NONNA: Do you know what I was thinking this morning? I don't like the Holy Mass anymore. Not in English anyway. In the old days, with the Latin, you used to get the gist. Just the gist. And then you could fill in the rest with what you wanted. So if you'd been telling lies or something then the Epistle or the Gospel would be about not telling lies because God knows when you're telling lies. That way it meant something to everybody. You see, because one person would be feeling sorry for swearing and then perhaps another for stealing something, and all the time I would be feeling sorry because God had heard me telling lies. I didn't tell very many. But you get my drift. I mean, today, if the Priest starts talking about coveting thy neighbour's wife . . . what does that mean to me? The English spoils it. That's why I fall asleep if you want to know. No magic. (*As she speaks, she takes off her shoes and lights a cigarette.* ANASTASIA *scrabbles in the sand.*) What are you doing Anastasia? Show me. (ANASTASIA *smiles and produces three or four cockles.*) Cockles! (*She hands them to her.*) Thank you my darling. I'll have them for breakfast. (*Laughs, and is amused as she continues.*) With my dandelion and garlic.

ANASTASIA *roots about in the bags and finds a deflated beach ball. A large one. She takes it out and begins to inflate it.*

NONNA: The tide's coming in, I think. Is it? There's a story about a man, a King . . . who tried to stop it. The tide. (*Laughs.*) He tried to stop the tide coming in. He couldn't though. We can't now. It's all to do with the moon. Nature. (*A couple walk along the shore hand in hand, played by* JULIA *and* ALFREDO. LEONORA *watches them strangely.*) Nature is a woman, you see Anastasia. She makes everything happen. She makes everything happen and men use her. And even when men abuse her she just keeps on starting it all up, all over again. A woman with no memory and no morals. It's not true that women are weak. It's just that they make the same mistakes again and again. No. Men are weak. (*She extinguishes the cigarette. Speaks sadly, watching the couple:*) Is it getting colder, do you think? The sun's gone in.

ANASTASIA *has inflated the beach ball and throws it to her. It passes between them until* NONNA *completely misses an ambitious throw from* ANASTASIA *which bounces off in the direction of the couple. The man bends down to pick it up, smiles, and tosses the ball back to* ANASTASIA.

ANASTASIA: Thanks.

The couple stroll off. ANASTASIA *tries to throw the ball to* NONNA.

NONNA: No, darling. No more, I'm tired. (*Looks at her watch.*) We better go soon. You have school.

They begin to pack up.

(*Stoically:*) This is my life now. This beach. These walks. What will I do when you don't want to come anymore? Don't say it won't happen. One day you won't come anymore – that's all. I think about that time. When you're too big to want to spend time with me. That's the way of things.

Scene Eight

The past. England, 1932.
ALFREDO *and* JULIA.
JULIA *faces the audience with a saucepan which she stirs with a large wooden spoon.* ALFREDO *comes up behind her and starts kissing her neck.*

JULIA: Get off.

ALFREDO: No.

JULIA: Thought you were hungry.

ALFREDO: I am. (*Nibbles neck.*) Mmm. Delicious.

JULIA (*shivers*): You mustn't do that. (*Meaning please do that.*)

ALFREDO: I know.

JULIA: I can't concentrate on two things at once.

ALFREDO'S *hands come round to cup* JULIA's *breasts.*

ALFREDO: I lay awake last night, the whole night, trying to remember the feel of your breasts in my hands.

JULIA: Well, you could have lain awake the whole night feeling them. It's your choice.

His hands disappear. JULIA *smiles thinly and concentrates on stirring.*

JULIA: Do you still love her?

ALFREDO (*moving away. Struggling*): She's my wife.

JULIA: What does that mean?

ALFREDO: She had the girls. She got old having my children. Her stomach – you know – hundreds of tiny lines, little white fish. I did that.

JULIA: I'm not talking about guilt. I'm talking about love. Because if you do, Alfredo, I don't want you to stay here. I want you to go.

ALFREDO: I love you Julia. I look at you and then I look at her.

JULIA: And?

ALFREDO: She needs me. I need you. (*Frustrated:*) Se eri Italiano mi capiresti.

JULIA (*frustrated at his Italian*): Don't do that. (*She turns to him.*) Look, I have to know if there's a marriage. If there's something that works, that's alive, then . . . (*Turns back.*) then I don't want you to come here.

ALFREDO *lays his head on her shoulder. Pauses.*

ALFREDO: How do you tell? In the bed, you know, there's nothing. For her. For me. Nothing. With you . . . Look, my hands, they're trembling.

JULIA *is weeping a little.* ALFREDO *touches her eyes.*

ALFREDO (*gently*): Hey! (*He tastes his fingers.*) What are you doing? You want to put some more salt in the sauce? Is that it?

She sobs and grins at the same time.

ALFREDO: Your taste. I can taste you for days after we've been together.

He puts his feet under hers and they begin to dance around the room. She leaning back into him, still carrying the saucepan.

JULIA: This is really hot, you know.

ALFREDO: Put it down.

JULIA *hands the saucepan to* NONNA *who remains on stage throughout.*

NONNA: I could smell her off him for days. Perfume. I couldn't afford perfume.

ALFREDO *and* JULIA *enjoy dancing together.*

ALFREDO: We only have one shadow.

JULIA: Where? We haven't got a shadow.

ALFREDO: I know, but if we did have, we'd only have one!

JULIA: You're a twit.

ALFREDO: Yes.

They kiss.

NONNA: She was a sly bitch, a bit of glamour painted on. Bait. Like a juicy worm, flesh with a hook through.

She demonstrates by making a ring with one hand and poking a finger through.

JULIA: You know, before you arrive, I promise myself it's for the last time. How long can this go on? Stolen moments. Furtive. Awful. But then I see you and I don't know why, I melt. I don't want to need you but I do, I long for you.

ALFREDO: I know. For me too. I try to stop. But I can't. You're my thrill, Julia.

JULIA: My lover.

ALFREDO: I love it when you talk like that.

JULIA: I love you. When you leave my life stops. That's the truth.

ALFREDO: When I leave my life stops.

JULIA: Then don't leave me. Leave her.

Scene Nine

The past. England, 1939. The Mare House.
The bed. LEONORA, ALFREDO, darkness. Rustling. ALFREDO lights a bedside lamp and roots about for a cigarette. He gets out of bed, appears very piqued. LEONORA lies face down into the pillows. ALFREDO clears his throat and sighs repeatedly, forcing the smoke out through his teeth. LEONORA sandwiches her head between top and bottom pillows, as if to shut off the light and his bitterness.

ALFREDO: Why do you punish me like this, Leonora, Hmm? You know I can't sleep. That I don't. Night after night beside you. Nothing. I tremble. Do you know that? I shake. (*Checks his hands.*) The frustration. Is it so much to ask?

Minutes. To give a few minutes of yourself to let me sleep peacefully? It's what tortures me – that for a few minutes of your bed I could sleep the whole night. It's a sin. To deny me. I hope you confess it.

LEONORA (*through the pillows*): I'll confess my sins. You confess yours.

ALFREDO: What!

LEONORA: You heard me. And don't shout, you'll wake the children.

ALFREDO: I'd like to know what you mean by that?

LEONORA: Oh please, don't bother.

ALFREDO: No. I'd like to know what you meant by that remark?

He tries to yank the pillow off her head. She clings onto it.

LEONORA: Please just leave me alone.

ALFREDO: Me! Me! Me! That's all you think about. Io! io! io!

LEONORA (*wounded, sarcastic*): Certo sicura eh! sicuro.

ALFREDO: Don't speak to me like that. (*He lifts the pillows.*) I know what you're thinking! Like you're some bloody saint. (*Thumps the pillow.*) Well you're fucking not! You try! You try selling amusement machines when there's a fucking war breaking out. And that's another thing. Those bastardi. They'll lock me up, you know, they could intern me. And yet still (*Thumping the pillow.*) you do this.

GIOIA (*off*): Mamma?

LEONORA: I hope you're satisfied. (*Sits up and calls to the child.*) It's all right Gioia. It's all right. Go back to sleep, darling. (*To ALFREDO:*) You only have to look at me and I get pregnant. My insides are like broken glass from you. That poor child calling me – born with the rent man at the bottom of the stairs shouting at Theresa for his money and where were you? On business. On business! Business that costs us money.

ALFREDO: Don't start.

LEONORA: And now I manage to scrape together enough to feed us and to clothe us and you want me to confess. You talk about minutes! (*Sighs.*) You talk about minutes. Oh yes.

ALFREDO: You don't have to get pregnant. We could just – uh – cuddle.

LEONORA: Alfredo, there's money in the tin. Why don't you go and buy a cuddle?

He hits her. She puts her hand to her lip.

ALFREDO: You made me do that.

LEONORA: There are all kinds of whoring – pay with pound notes, pay in kind. No different. It's a whore.

ALFREDO: You made me do that.

LEONORA: You made me old and ugly. What's a drop of blood?

ALFREDO: Don't blame me. You let yourself go. There's no need.

LEONORA: You're right. It's easy to be beautiful. Take away the children and the work and the worry and the lies and the humiliations and it's the simplest thing in the world to be beautiful. Or love. Everyone who is loved is beautiful. Easy.

ALFREDO: I do love you. But you won't let me. How can I love you when you won't let me?

LEONORA: I refuse to cry. I'm not going to cry any more for you. I promised myself.

ALFREDO: You'd like me to go, wouldn't you? You want me to leave you?

LEONORA: Do what you like, Alfredo. You will anyway.

GIOIA (*off*): Mamma, I can't sleep.

LEONORA (*opening the door*): Ssh now – you'll wake the others. Go to sleep.

She closes the door and slowly slides down it, the entire length, finishing crouched on the floor, her face in her hands. ALFREDO starts to scratch his head violently, helplessly. The silence is punctuated only by huge sobs from LEONORA.

ALFREDO (*crooning*): Hey Mamma, don't cry, Ssh. Don't cry. It's OK. I'm not going anywhere. Ssh. I'm not going. Don't cry, eh?

He starts to kiss her head again,

whispering, until eventually she looks up and he kisses her eyes and then the blood on her lips.

ALFREDO: Mamma. Come on. Let's go to bed. Eh? Sshh.

He helps her up and half carries her to the bed.
He puts out the light. They embrace in the dark. He moves on top of her.

ALFREDO: I love you. It's OK. It's OK.

GIOIA (*off*): Mamma!

Long pause. Rustling. ALFREDO groans. Long pause.

GIOIA (*off*): Mamma.

LEONORA *goes to disentangle herself from the embrace.* ALFREDO *pulls her back. Determined.*

GIOIA (*off*): Mamma!

ALFREDO (*thwarted*): Ma Porco Dio!

Scene Ten

The past. England, 1939.
The bed. ALFREDO *packing.*
LEONORA *sitting.* JULIA *pacing. The scene is played as if the two dialogues are being delivered independently.* NONNA *sits on the bed.*

JULIA: The hours and hours I have wasted. Waiting by telephones. Waiting for you to call me. Not knowing whether you were leaving or staying or what.

ALFREDO: I know.

LEONORA: Night after night. Not a whisper, could have been dead all of us for all you knew.

GIOIA (*off*): Mamma . . .

JULIA: Fredo, I don't want you to come to me, not dragging your guilt behind you. I don't want that dragging us down.

ALFREDO: I know.

LEONORA: Don't stay out of charity, Alfredo. I won't have you pitying me.

ALFREDO: I know.

LEONORA: I pity her if you want to know.

NONNA: You're a sick man.

LEONORA: Only a sick man would desert his family for a slut. I pity her. She must be simple. (*Tapping her forehead.*)

JULIA: I will not be your vice. I will not be your sin. I will not be confessed! If you're ashamed of me, give me up. No! If you're ashamed of me I'll give you up!

ALFREDO: I know.

LEONORA:
NONNA: I know. You always say
JULIA: that.

JULIA: As if it explained everything.

NONNA: As if it was enough.

ALFREDO: What am I supposed to say?

LEONORA:
NONNA: Don't say anything.
JULIA:

ANASTASIA (*off*): Gran?

LEONORA: Do you pity me?

JULIA: Do you really want to be with me? Well? Yes or no?

ALFREDO: No! Yes! No! Look, I do love you. I do. I do love you. Believe me.

LEONORA:
NONNA: And what about her?
JULIA:

LEONORA: Do you tell *her* you love her?

JULIA: Do you tell her you love her?

ALFREDO: No!

ANASTASIA (*off*): Granny?

JULIA *and* LEONORA *speak together*:

JULIA: Because if you do, Fredo, you can take your charm and your lap-dog eyes and your shrugs and your vows and your promises and your blasted operas . . . because I will not be treated as if I were a simpleton or an object . . .

LEONORA: I don't believe you, you would say no to anything to wriggle your way out of trouble . . . you would agree, to anything . . . your lies, you're a terrible liar! Am I supposed to swallow your trumped-up excuses night after night? Do you think I'm an ornament?

ALFREDO (*cutting them off*): Look! I can't hear myself think! The thing is – I look at her (*Looks at them both.*) and then I look at you.

He looks at them both.

LEONORA:
NONNA: And?
JULIA:

ALFREDO (*reaches inside his suitcase and starts to produce bingo balls*): On the red: number five. Kelly's Eye: number one. Clickety-click: sixty six. Me and you: number two.

ANASTASIA (*off*): Granny!

NONNA *seems to hear* ANASTASIA *for the first time, gets up from the bed and leaves the room.*

Scene Eleven

The past. England. JULIA's *flat.*
ALFREDO *sits with* JULIA *on the bed. He takes some clothes out of the suitcase.*

JULIA: And the children? Did you say goodbye?

ALFREDO: Yes, I said goodbye. Of course I said goodbye. Everyone was crying. I walked down the stairs and out of the door and the noise was like a thousand seagulls flying above my head. It was the worst thing I ever did.

JULIA *lays back on the bed.*

JULIA: Thanks.

ALFREDO: What?

JULIA: Forget it.

She begins putting his clothes back into the suitcase.

ALFREDO: What are you doing?

JULIA: If it was the worst thing you ever did then don't do it. Everything with you is so *loud*, so . . . (*She can't find the word.*) Seagulls! It's not Verdi. You know . . . you've left your wife. You wanted to, that's all.

ALFREDO: She said she'd kill herself, that she'd kill them all.

JULIA: Well yes! I'm sure she does feel pretty badly about it. What did you expect? Flowers?

ALFREDO: No.

JULIA: I'm just trying to say it's unlikely she will actually kill anybody. I don't know, I suppose she *is* capable of killing me.

ALFREDO: Oh yes. She could kill you.

JULIA (*considering*): You could have brought the children.

ALFREDO: No.

JULIA: No. Stupid.

ALFREDO (*breaking down during this*): Theresa told me, she said I was, she said I'd ruined their lives and that I was a bad man. My own daughter. Twelve years old.

JULIA: Oh my darling . . . (*They kiss, she strokes his head.*) Poor baby. I was thinking . . . You have so many shirts. Where am I going to put them all? (*She smiles. He smiles. Pause.*) Look . . . they'll . . . Theresa is bound to be upset, all of them. Don't torture yourself. Maybe in time they'll be able to see it from your . . .

ALFREDO (*interrupting her*): Please, can we not talk about it anymore. I don't want to think about it anymore.

ALFREDO *starts to kiss up her leg. Under the cover.*

JULIA: Don't.

ALFREDO *grunts.*

JULIA: Christ.

ALFREDO (*out of desperation*): I need to remind myself why I left.

JULIA (*hurt*): Uh? And it's there, is it?

ALFREDO *continues.*

JULIA (*trying to push him away*): Don't! Christ! And what about me Alfredo, huh? Why've I . . . I mean . . . What do I get? Stories of how Leonora didn't understand you or excite you, of her stretch marks, the fat on her thighs. Hmm? What if my legs get fat? Christ! I said what if my legs? . . .

Scene Twelve

The present. England. Beach.
Seagulls. Child's sandpit. NONNA *and* ANASTASIA *are making sandcastles using little shaped buckets and spades. Neither wears shoes.*

NONNA: It's strange. When that whore took your grandfather away from me, I took to wearing black. I didn't know what to do . . . and Theresa had to do everything. She was like a father to your mother. I was stupid. I would have given him everything each time he came back. But Theresa made me give her the keys to the cash box. She was thirteen. Whenever your grandfather came home she used to leave him an allowance on the mantelpiece, and that was all she would let him have. Two pounds every week. On the mantelpiece. I couldn't bear to see that. See him humiliated like that. I used to take the money off the mantelpiece and put it in his wallet, and put a few shillings into his pocket too. Not for anything really, but just so he could pretend that it was his own money. I was wrong though. It didn't keep him with me. One day he just stopped coming. After we left the café under the railway bridge I only saw him two more times. Walking up the aisle with his daughters. One after the other . . . as if nothing had happened. He was a charming man. I always loved him. Everybody loved him. I do now. I forgave him for everything years ago . . . years ago . . . let me tell you something: I didn't know anything about anything. Not even after we got married. No one ever told me anything . . . I didn't know how to please him in that way. So you see. I blame myself for everything. Not him. I never saw him naked. In all those years I never saw him naked.

JULIA *and* ALFREDO *walk across the sandcastles, destroying them.*

ANASTASIA: Hey!

JULIA *and* ALFREDO *walk straight into the section with* EDUARDO. ANASTASIA's *'Hey' comes seconds before* EDUARDO's *'Imbecile'!*

64   A LITTLE LIKE DROWNING

Scene Thirteen

The past. England, 1941. Eduardo Mare's House.
Dim light of a study. EDUARDO, ALFREDO's *father, is seated in a big leather armchair.* ALFREDO *wears a raincoat, and stands, or rather paces, irritated and embarrassed by his father's tirade.* JULIA *sits, remote, on a wooden chair, smoking.*

EDUARDO: Imbecile! Vieni qui da me con questa donna a chiedermi la mia benedizione? E le tue figle? Ti credi di poter . . ? [You fool! You come to me with this woman to ask for my blessing? In this adultery? And what about your daughters? Do you think you can just . . . ?]

ALFREDO (*cutting in*): Papá . . . Non e necessario dirmi quello che ho fatto. Lo so . . . [You don't have to tell me what I've done – I know]

EDUARDO: Non m'interromperre! Come osi! Ho messo al mondo due figli patetici! Uno semina bastardi a dritta e a marica, e l'altro un volgarissimo gaga! Ma che Papá e Papá! [Don't interrupt me! How dare you? Two pathetic sons I've produced. One of them siring bastards right, left and centre and the other a waster and a nothing. Don't 'Papá' me!]

ALFREDO: Talk in English, papá.

EDUARDO: I'll talk in English all right! What do you want me to say in English different to my Italian? Fine? Marvellous? Talk in English!

ALFREDO: Look papá. We didn't have to come here.

EDUARDO: Then why did you? Don't tell me you were being polite. You wanted me to be introduced? Is that it? Hello. Goodbye.

ALFREDO: Papá, I need money. I have debts. I owe money here and there . . . not much. I can pay it back, but I need a little to get started. Just to see me right for a few . . .

EDUARDO (*interrupting*): Don't crawl, Alfredo. It sickens me. Tell me how much you want and get out of my sight.

ALFREDO: You don't understand do you? You think luck plays no part in this? With some luck, just a little, I wouldn't be here now. Everybody has bad breaks . . . if it hadn't been for the war I might have been a rich man by now. Some of my ideas . . .

EDUARDO (*interrupting*): Ideas! Ideas! Hai la mania delle idee [You're sick with ideas]

JULIA: Mr Mare, if you'll let Alfredo have this money, I promise you we shan't trouble you again. We're leaving for Ireland tonight. (*Turns to* ALFREDO:) Alfredo?

ALFREDO: She's right, papá. I won't be back for more . . . Papá?

EDUARDO *takes out a cheque book and begins to write.*

EDUARDO (*emotionless*): I'm not your papá. When you take this you stop being my son. The ring on her finger, is she already married?

JULIA: My husband died.

EDUARDO (*hands the cheque to* ALFREDO): I haven't put in a number. Let your own conscience decide how much you take from me.

JULIA *gets up to go. She offers a hand to* EDUARDO.

JULIA: Goodbye.

EDUARDO *ignores her.*

ALFREDO: Papá. Please. Try and understand.

EDUARDO *deliberately turns his head away and spits on the floor.*

Scene Fourteen

The beach. The present.

NONNA: What was I doing? Uh, do you know how I knew he'd really gone? I was thinking about him – he used to sing a lot – and – he loved opera and I went to put on one of his gramophone records and he'd taken them. They'd all gone. But by the gramophone was his cigarette case and it had one cigarette in it. So I smoked it.

ACT TWO

Scene One

The past. Dublin, 1945. ALFREDO *and* JULIA's *house. The house is in Dublin. A table laid for three.*

JULIA: She's not coming.

ALFREDO: Of course she's coming.

JULIA: Will you ring the guest house and see if she's left?

ALFREDO: Darling . . .

JULIA: What?

ALFREDO: Don't . . . (*Thinks better of it.*) . . . Nothing.

JULIA (*fragile*): I've cooked lamb. You said she'd like that.

ALFREDO: Yes, she loves it. Yes! At any rate she always used to. Smells marvellous. With vegetables.

JULIA: Yes.

ALFREDO: She won't have eaten lamb for a while, I bet.

JULIA: You should have collected her.

ALFREDO: I told her to take a taxi. I arranged that with Mrs McGoldrick.

JULIA: I have to pick Peter up at ten.

ALFREDO: Oh. Why?

JULIA: Why? Well, because I thought that Gioia would have gone by then and because you know he won't sleep and anyway it's not fair just to dump him. That's why.

ALFREDO: I suppose not but I don't understand this not sleeping business . . . the girls all slept like bears. You think it's natural?

JULIA: What are you saying? That I'm not a good mother?

ALFREDO: Christ!

JULIA: Well what?

ALFREDO: I wasn't talking about you. I was talking about Peter.

JULIA: No. You were talking about babies and them sleeping and that your babies with Leonora all slept well. Maybe her milk was better than my milk. Or what?

ALFREDO: Don't be ridiculous. Anyway, Italian women – it's their vocation. It's in their blood. They feel naked without a child at the nipple or in the belly. It's a racial thing.

JULIA: Sometimes, Fredo, I think you're very dim, you know, because you can hurt so casually – like someone with great flapping feet always kicking shins or, I don't know, treading on everybody. I don't think you mean to.

ALFREDO: I don't understand you when you get like this. You're nervous, aren't you? Of Gioia?

JULIA: I expect so.

ALFREDO: Me too.

JULIA: I'm terrified she'll hate me. I wouldn't blame her. I think I'd hate me.

ALFREDO: If she's rude it's her mother talking. But anyway she won't be, I'm sure. She doesn't know about you.

JULIA: O come on! She knows. Because you all pretend I don't exist doesn't mean they don't know.

ALFREDO: Please Julia, don't do this. Don't be like this.

JULIA: Well I'm nervous, you see, of your daughter. I'd like her to like me. And she won't. But I still have to try, and I still have to smile, and I know that you don't feel you can help. And I'm nervous. That's all.

ALFREDO: I love you.

JULIA: And I love you. And the food's going to be ruined. And it's probably a racial thing with Italian women that they cook better than me too. (*Smiles ruefully.*) Oh, by the way, Peter said Mam again today. And 'burd'.

ALFREDO: What's burd?

JULIA: A thing that flies, I think.

LEONORA: That boy's going to be a singer . . . Have you heard him laugh? Very musical.

JULIA: His yelling's not so bad either.

Doorbell.

JULIA: Who's going to go?

ALFREDO: I should really, because

officially you don't live here.

JULIA: Where *do* I live officially?

ALFREDO: I don't know.

JULIA: Fine. Well, work on that, will you?

Doorbell.

JULIA (*to* ALFREDO *as he goes out*): In which case who's cooked?

ALFREDO: You have. That's all right.

JULIA: Oh have I? How nice. And what about the make-up in the bathroom? Is that yours?

ALFREDO (*off*): I moved it.

JULIA (*nodding*): You moved it. Good. Fine.

Greetings off. JULIA *prepares herself.* ALFREDO *returns with* GIOIA. GIOIA *is 14.*

ALFREDO: Apparently, uh Gioia's been washing her hair . . .

JULIA: Ah, pretty.

ALFREDO: Which explains . . .

JULIA: Yes. Never mind . . .

ALFREDO: Darling, I know you've seen Mrs Jarrett before, but I don't know if you've been properly introduced.

GIOIA: Never.

JULIA: No. Silly, isn't it? I'm Julia. And you're Gioia.

GIOIA: Yes.

JULIA: Yes. Golly you've uh . . . (*Nodding, smiling.*) You've grown. I'm pleased to meet you. You were . . . (*She shows a height with her hand.*)

GIOIA *smiles politely.*

JULIA: Well, I expect you must be famished. All this sightseeing.

GIOIA: I've eaten, thank you.

JULIA: Oh? Really?

ALFREDO: I did say we'd eat together, darling.

GIOIA: I know, Papá, but.

ALFREDO: But what?

GIOIA: Well, I was hungry and I thought that perhaps you might have forgotten

you'd said that . . . you know like . . . well, Christmas and things.

ALFREDO: Darling, I don't think Christmas has really got anything to do with dinner tonight. And Julia's cooked you lamb. When was the last time you ate lamb?

JULIA: It doesn't matter, really. Would you just like some tea?

ALFREDO: What about having the meat by itself?

GIOIA: Yes, if you like.

ALFREDO: In a sandwich, eh?

GIOIA: Thank you.

ALFREDO: Because Papá hasn't eaten and you wouldn't want to sit and watch us stuffing ourselves, would you?

GIOIA: No.

JULIA: Well we could perhaps eat later on, Fredo, then Gioia might have, might be more interested in food.

ALFREDO (*irritated*): Oh OK. (*To* GIOIA:) I think you would have been all right to eat a sandwich, wouldn't you?

GIOIA: Yes, of course.

JULIA (*firmly*): That's settled then. Lamb sandwiches later on.

ALFREDO *raises his eyebrows at* GIOIA *who smiles.* ALFREDO *smiles.*

JULIA (*as cheerfully as she can manage*): What? Have I said something funny?

ALFREDO: No. Nothing. (*He smiles.*)

Pause.

JULIA: Your father tells me you went to the zoo today. Was that nice?

GIOIA: Yes thank you.

ALFREDO: We had great fun, didn't we?

GIOIA: Yes.

ALFREDO: The gorilla! (*Makes a face, beats his chest.*) Ugh! Ugh!

Pause.

JULIA: What's your favourite animal?

GIOIA: The duckbilled platypus.

JULIA: Oh. I didn't know they had any.

GIOIA: They haven't.

JULIA: But, still, you like them.

GIOIA: Yes. There was one in a story Mamma used to tell us. Remember Papá?

ALFREDO (*not remembering*): Yes!

JULIA: I see. Are you fond of stories?

GIOIA: Yes.

JULIA: Yes. Me too. Very fond of them.

Silence. JULIA *produces a cardboard box.*

JULIA: By the way, uh, I came across some rather pretty frocks recently and we thought they might . . . they're terribly sweet. I just hope they're the right size. There's one each. Would you like to try yours on?

ALFREDO: Of course she would. These are beautiful dresses. For a princess. Put it on and then we can have a fashion parade, eh? You could be a mannequin, eh Julia? So slim and pretty.

JULIA: Yes. Very pretty. Young lady.

GIOIA: It seems a bit unfair.

JULIA: What's that now?

GIOIA: Doesn't matter.

ALFREDO: What's unfair?

GIOIA: Oh, I don't know!

ALFREDO: Well what did you say it for?

GIOIA: Well, that I should get a dress and a holiday and Theresa gets nothing and has to work and she could have gone to the Academy but Mamma said the uniform was too expensive.

JULIA: I bought Theresa a dress, too, actually.

GIOIA: What? School uniform? Grey?

ALFREDO (*exploding*): It had nothing to do with the cost of a uniform! Of course the money for a uniform could have been found, it goes without saying. I would have gone without personally had it just been a matter of a uniform! Yes, it's too complex to expect you to understand. You see, Daddy had to come to Dublin because of the war and then

– do you know how much the fees would have been?

JULIA *tries to intervene.*

Ma lasscia stare! Eo! sto parlando! (*Returning to Gioia.*) And what about you? Couldn't pay for both of you, could I? (*To* JULIA:) It had nothing to do with the uniform. I don't know where she's had that idea from. (*Pause.*) That's in the past anyway.

GIOIA: The war's over. We had a street party when it finished.

JULIA: Would you like to try the frock on? (*She hands* GIOIA *the box.*)

GIOIA: Is there a bathroom or . . . ?

JULIA: Yes, I'll show you.

ALFREDO: No, don't you go. You're a guest. (*To* GIOIA:) I'll take you darling. And isn't that good you can take a present back for Theresa? We'll have to find something else for her too. What do you think she'd like?

GIOIA (*exiting*): I've bought her a cigarette lighter with a picture of St Patrick on.

ALFREDO (*exiting*): Brava.

JULIA *sits, pensively. Lights a cigarette.* ALFREDO *returns.*

ALFREDO (*cheerfully*): You do fuss! She would have eaten the food. I'm starving. It's her age to be awkward.

JULIA: Is it true about Theresa?

ALFREDO: True? What? That she had a place at the Academy? Look, Julia, it's their mother talking . . . spite . . . I don't blame her. It's hard for us all. I'd love a new suit. I'm sure there are things you need. A couple of years and Theresa'll be wanting to get married, Academy or no Academy. Anyway.

JULIA: Anyway.

ALFREDO: Isn't she beautiful, eh? My girl. I can't believe how beautiful she is. Like a peach.

JULIA (*sad*): Yes, she's remarkable. And Gioia's quite right. The war's over. Will you go back to England?

ALFREDO: I'll go and carve the lamb, shall I?

JULIA: Yes, Alfredo, you go and carve.

ALFREDO: Gioia . . . It's probably . . . I mean she lives in a different world. She's probably in a love affair. That's it. She's probably in love with some French sailor. Don't be . . . uh . . .

JULIA: Yes, I'm sure that's what's wrong with her.

GIOIA *returns.*

GIOIA (*to* JULIA): Thank you. It's very pretty.

ALFREDO: Well, why haven't you got it on?

GIOIA: It didn't fit.

JULIA (*snapping*): I'll see to the food. (*She goes out quickly.*)

GIOIA: I'll have to get mamma to alter it a little. Then it'll be lovely, thank you.

ALFREDO (*shouting*): It's only adjustments, Julia! Then it'll be lovely! (*To* GIOIA:) Why didn't you say that? (*To* JULIA, *loudly:*) She says it's perfect.

JULIA (*off*): Lovely.

ALFREDO (*to* GIOIA. *Angry, hard*): Now you go in and say thank you, properly, to Mrs Jarrett! Not every day somebody gives you a new dress is it? Now you go in there, you give her a kiss and you say thank you! Per me! Hai capito? You could help her with the food.

GIOIA (*distressed, anxious*): OK. (*She puts down the box, hugs him. A child exits.*)

ALFREDO (*relieved*): Good. Marvellous. (*To the women off:*) Tell you something. I could eat a whole sheep if you're not hungry.

He pours himself a glass of wine and begins to hum and sing a romantic Italian song. GIOIA *comes through with a vegetable tureen.*

ALFREDO: Remember this? (*He sings the chorus line. He gestures for her to join in.* GIOIA *nods, joins in hesitantly, then happily. They sing noisily.* JULIA *comes in. The Mares are singing at the tops of their voices in Italian.*)

JULIA: Lovely. What is it you're singing?

They sing.

JULIA: Fredo?

They sing and clap.

JULIA (*helpless*): Fredo?

They sing and clap.
JULIA *goes out.*

Scene Two

*The past. The Mare cafe. Kitchen.
The present. The beach.*
JULIA, ALFREDO *and* GIOIA *leave the stage, but do not clear the table.*
THERESA *and* FATHER DAVID COGAN *replace them at the table,* FR DAVID *bringing with him a plate of almost eaten spaghetti with a red sauce and a red mouth and napkin with a red stain. He finishes his spaghetti as* NONNA *comes onto the beach. She is looking for* ANASTASIA. *The past and the beach present are played simultaneously.*

NONNA: Anastasia! Anastasia! Ach. (*She sits wearily on the beach and starts fishing around in her bags for a bottle of sherry.*) Anastasia, I haven't got time to be playing around. It's late. There'll be customers and no hot water. I can't carry all these bags up the hill. Ach, I'm mad. I'm seventy-three (*Puffs.*) I could retire. I could ask for what I wanted from your dad. I started the business. It's in my name. Oh yes, the deeds are in my name; not in the name of Powell, in the name of Mare. You ask your papá. You all forget that don't you? Well I don't.

FR DAVID: Ah, God bless you Theresa: that's a wonderful plate of spaghetti and no mistake. Cheers. Now, Leonora, what's worrying you? The little shop? You want me to help with the washing-up, is that it?

NONNA: The little café – white front, shutters . . . and a few tables: four or five, can't remember. Not like now, eh darling? (*Looks round.*) Anastasia! (*Puffs, irritable.*) Ah managia miseria.

FR DAVID: Gioia? Ah, it seems only yesterday she was making her first Holy Communion. Sixteen? Is she now? Ah yes, she will be. Little cherub . . . sixteen, you say? Time flies. Ah, dear me yes, time flies. Marvellous drop of wine.

THERESA: Mamma?

LEONORA: What?

THERESA: Are you going to speak to Father about Gioia or what?

FR DAVID: Goodness! What's the poor child done?

NONNA (*on the beach*): I used to worry. No father to keep an eye on them. I used to be sick with worry. And Gioia was such an imp. Always one for the boys. Always crying over somebody. I used to insist they always wore their knickers. Even in bed. They always wore their knickers. Stupid.

FR DAVID: A love letter, Theresa? What does it say? Can I read it?

THERESA: She's got it. She's upstairs in her bedroom refusing to come out.

FR DAVID: And you know this fellow, Theresa?

THERESA: Vaguely. He comes in the shop.

FR DAVID: Is he Catholic?

THERESA: Yes, but that's not the point.

FR DAVID: Well, it's a start.

THERESA: I mean, of course it's the point, Father, but he's still a man and he's still capable of getting her into trouble, isn't he? And mam's not sleeping over it.

NONNA: Theresa used to get so anxious. Up half the night.

FR DAVID: Gregory Powell! Oh, I know him! He's a nice enough lad. Harmless. He's in the Guild of St Stephen.

NONNA: The priest was a fool. Well either a fool or very wise, I could never make up my mind. He's dead now, God rest him. But he was a real priest. Not like the ones you get now. Folk guitars and free love.

FR DAVID (*to* LEONORA): I'm sorry, I didn't catch what you said.

LEONORA: I said belonging to the Guild of St Stephen doesn't stop him slobbering over Gioia.

THERESA: Mamma!

FR DAVID: No, your mother's quite right. (*To* LEONORA:) What is it you'd like me to do? I'm not the boy's father.

LEONORA: And I'm not Gioia's. That's the problem.

THERESA: Can't you speak with her, Father? Both of them? Put Mamma's mind at rest?

FR DAVID: This letter. You found it, you say?

THERESA: Yes. In her pillowslip.

FR DAVID: And it's uh provocative, or what? Does he make suggestions?

THERESA: No father, he didn't write it. She wrote it to him.

FR DAVID: Uh – uh. So how now it was in *her* pillowslip, and not his?

THERESA: Well, I suppose, I don't know. I suppose she hadn't got round to sending it.

FR DAVID: Not urgent, then?

LEONORA: You know what men are like. And she's a child. Gullible. She'd believe anything. You know how easily impressed young girls are.

THERESA: Shall I tell Father what it said?

LEONORA: No!

FR DAVID: She's upstairs, you say. I'll go up then, shall I?

LEONORA: No. I'll get her to come down.

She exits, taking some of the crockery with her.

THERESA: I'll do that Mamma. Leave it.

FR DAVID: Your poor mother. It's a tragedy. When I see these things I wonder why the Lord is so mysterious. That he strikes the innocent. Still, life is short and heaven is long.

THERESA *opens up a tin, takes out a ten shilling note and gives it to him.*

THERESA: Father, would you say Mass, please? For the family intentions.

FR DAVID: Of course, of course (*Refuses*

the money.) There's no need for that. Monday 7.30. I know that's free. Let me just write that in my little book here. The Mare family. (*Notes the feast day.*) Our Lady of Lourdes. All right?

LEONORA *brings in a sullen* GIOIA.

GIOIA: Father.

FR DAVID: Ah Gioia, how are you? Your mother was telling me you were sixteen.

GIOIA: Yes.

FR DAVID: God bless you, you'll all be getting married soon.

LEONORA: We'll leave you two.

They exit. FR DAVID *nods and smiles weakly to them.*

We'll just have a little chinwag, eh Gioia? The two of us?

GIOIA: If you like.

FR DAVID (*to the departing women*): Splendid. Good. (*Pause.*) So I gather there's some problem with a letter?

GIOIA: It's not a problem for me.

FR DAVID: Gregory Powell, what do you see in him now? He looks like a labrador.

GIOIA: I know. I don't like him anymore. He's a drip.

FR DAVID: Yes he is. God forgive me for saying it. He's not even in the parish soccer team. (*Delighted.*) What do you mean you don't like him any more?

GIOIA: Well, I did like him but I don't anymore. He's not even in the soccer team.

FR DAVID: Exactly. So we're agreed on that, are we? He's not suitable.

GIOIA: Not in the least.

FR DAVID: Grand. Now then, this letter. Can I see?

GIOIA: No. It's stupid. It's really childish. I wrote it weeks ago.

FR DAVID: Ah, I've written one or two of those in my life.

GIOIA: Don't believe you.

FR DAVID: It's the truth. When I was at school I was class poet. Wrote anything for anybody. One penny per sonnet. Or

tobacco. The lies I wrote for a penny. You know, lot of romantic hogwash neatly written. (*Laughs,* GIOIA *too.*)

GIOIA: The thing is, Father. I'm not a child any more and I know that if Papa were here there wouldn't be any of this fuss every time I have a friend.

FR DAVID: Yes, I know.

GIOIA (*thrown*): Oh, well, tell Theresa that, and Mamma.

FR DAVID: You think they need reminding?

GIOIA: Yes! (*Pause.*) No. (*Pause.*) No. (*Pause.*)

FR DAVID (*into preaching mode*): You see, you can be in love with a person and you can be in love with love. No matter what your age. D'you see? Now that's great fun but dangerous. And that's why there's the sacrament of marriage to protect you . . . to give you a foundation.

GIOIA: You mean like my parents?

FR DAVID: Gioia. (*Sighs.*) You light ten candles, one goes out . . . I don't know why . . . and anyway, I'm sure your father will come home. One day he'll snap to his senses. That's my feeling. I pray for it. (*Pause.*) Do you hear from him ever?

GIOIA: Oh, sometimes. He sends 'sorry' postcards. Sorry I missed your birthday, sorry I forgot Christmas, sorry to hear you were sick.

FR DAVID: Try not to be bitter.

GIOIA (*meaning it*): I'm not. He's got a terrible memory. He's such a . . . you know, all over the place. And I think SHE probably doesn't remind him.

FR DAVID: Very likely. So, talking of letters. What about a little deal, eh? You give me the letter to the labrador and I'll promise I'll burn it without reading it. Then everyone will be happy. How about that?

GIOIA: Really?

FR DAVID: But listen now, that's between me and thee, though? No blabbing.

GIOIA: No blabbing.

FR DAVID: Grand.

She gives him the letter.

To the fires. (*He sets light to the letter.*)

NONNA (*back on the beach.*

ANASTASIA *enters*): He gave your poor mother such a shaking. Made her read the letter out loud to him. I remember her face afterwards, all blotchy, red eyed. (*Shakes her head.*)

The letter is burnt.

GIOIA: Thank you.

FR DAVID: Not at all.

They begin to exit.

FR DAVID: Now – let's think what we can say to your poor mother.

NONNA: The letter, of course, it was to your stupid father. They were married a couple of years later. So stupid. All the fuss and tears and the . . . and then within a few years both girls were married.

Scene Three

The past. England, 1950. Pre, during and post wedding reception.
GIOIA's *wedding reception.* BRUNO, *her uncle, is setting up to take a photograph of the bride with her father.*

ALFREDO: Isn't she beautiful? Two men crying in the church for her.

BRUNO: Fantastic.

GIOIA: Oh papá, shut up!

ALFREDO: What do you mean, shut up? It's true. No, OK, not two, three. Your father crying too. Floods. Great baby.

She kisses him. He beams.

GIOIA: I'm not beautiful and you know it. Why do you always say that I am?

BRUNO: Shut up you both and keep still.

GIOIA: I've got your nose for a start.

ALFREDO: Nothing wrong with this nose. (*He feels his.*) It's been in the family for generations, eh Bruno? (*Laughs.*) It was good enough for our mamma and her mamma and her mamma and it's good enough for you! (*He tweaks hers.*)

GIOIA: Well I hope I don't pass it on.

BRUNO: You will.

GIOIA: Greg's is much nicer.

ALFREDO: Ach Greg!

GIOIA: What's that supposed to mean?

ALFREDO: Well, if his nose is so wonderful how come he's so keen to marry yours?

BRUNO: I don't think it's her nose he's after!

GIOIA (*drily*): Ha Ha.

BRUNO: Aspetta fino a stasera. Eh, Bimbo? (*He's saying 'Wait till tonight'. He thinks that's funny. He sings.*) La signora che fa cosi. Bocca bocca la notte e il dí. (*Makes a sexual gesture.*)

ALFREDO: Eh! Ma stai t'zit.

GIOIA: Hurry up, Uncle. I've got to go in.

BRUNO: Listen, you keep these for a lifetime. Give me a minute to make them, eh?

GIOIA: Well, at least take some with Greg and mamma in, too! Where is she? Theresa! Theresa! Dov'é mamma?

THERESA: What?

GIOIA: We want mamma in this.

THERESA: I'll call her. Don't be long. They want papá to sing.

ALFREDO: Eh! Sing nothing.

GIOIA: Yes!

ALFREDO: I can't sing any more.

GIOIA: Not even for me?

ALFREDO: Oh, for you . . . maybe . . . later maybe.

LEONORA *appears. Husband and wife briefly together. Both silent, awkward. A beat.*

LEONORA: Who wants me?

BRUNO: Me. Leonora. I want you.

GIOIA: Come here mamma and have your photograph taken.

LEONORA: Don't be silly.

THERESA (*following up*): Don't *you* be silly. Do as you're told, and *please*, Uncle Bruno, hurry up! Greg and his family are waiting to start.

BRUNO: Hurry! Hurry! Hurry! What's the matter with everyone? OK, hurry, hurry. Smile . . . watch the blackbird.

THERESA *suddenly throws confetti all over them. Howls and shrieks.*

BRUNO: Wonderful! Fantastic!

The whole company close, elated by the event, burst into a song. Paesano, Italian, wonderful, stamping of feet. They can be close in song without explanation but when it finishes there is a space again . . . and awkwardness.

BRUNO (*embracing* ALFREDO): My brother.

ALFREDO (*moved, sentimental*): Bruno, I would have emptied my pockets today, even if I had known it would take my last penny, just to have this moment . . . not for me, but for my wife and my children, my girls. (*Clears his throat. To the* PRIEST:) Even God cannot change the past. Not even God. For every dream goes wrong there is a new dream . . . All my life I've been in the shallows . . . (*Shrugs.*) Bogged down in the shallows, treading water . . . never enough to swim (*Laughs, gestures.*) but enough to drown. So I uh dream of oceans. I dream that my girls . . . my darlings . . . Theresa . . . Gioia . . . would each find good husbands, and now, at this moment, that dream comes true. And so (*Vacant. Lost.*) and so (*Weakly.*) Salut (*To* LEONORA.) Salut.

ALL: Salut!

VOICES OFF: Eh! Fredo! Bruno!

BRUNO: Coming! Coming!

They make their way inside.

BRUNO (*a clown*): I want to dance. Who wants to dance with me?

They all go off merrily, save ALFREDO *and* LEONORA *who stand apart and awkward. Dance music off.*

ALFREDO: A good day, eh?

LEONORA: Yes.

ALFREDO: Yes, marvellous. And the weather. This is the most beautiful spring I can remember.

They dance.

ALFREDO: How are you?

LEONORA: Fine. And you?

ALFREDO: Yes. Fine. I'm fine. And the café? Busy?

LEONORA: Yes, yes it's getting busy now.

ALFREDO: Right.

They dance.

ALFREDO: That girl. What a beauty she is!

LEONORA: She looks like you.

ALFREDO (*proud*): No!

LEONORA: Everyone says so. They always do.

ALFREDO: She's so young to be married. It breaks my heart.

LEONORA: He's a good man. He's steady.

ALFREDO (*nods*): You know what I thought today? What I remembered? Once when I, when I was home . . . years ago . . . she must have been eleven, twelve, I barged into the bathroom and she was washing herself. The door wasn't locked – not used, I suppose, to having a man about – anyway, she was standing at the basin. Nuda. Niente adosso. The light streaming in. And it was the most lovely thing I ever saw. Like a bud, Leonora, opening.

He's stopped dancing for this last, and on 'bud opening' makes a gesture of opening between thumb and fingers. They dance.

ALFREDO: And now she's married. It breaks my heart. What am I saying? I'm happy!

LEONORA: Yes.

ALFREDO: I want them all to be happy. You know that.

They dance.

ALFREDO: And you're fine, you say?

LEONORA: Yes. I'm so happy you were able to come . . . Alfredo . . .

ALFREDO: A man is blessed from God when he has such children.

LEONORA *weeps on his shoulder momentarily.*

ALFREDO (*embarrassed*): Yes, the most

beautiful spring I can remember.

·LEONORA: I expect you'll have to be going back? To Dublin?

ALFREDO (*rueful*): Yes. Tomorrow. Stupid really, but the suit. I hired it for the weekend. I'll have to uh . . .

LEONORA: Of course.

They dance.

Scene Three i

ANASTASIA *comes on.*

NONNA: Do you ever say a prayer for your poor grandfather?

ANASTASIA: Sometimes.

NONNA: Do you? Please do, darling. And for me. Pray for me, too. Prayers, you know, they're like savings. You can store them up for purgatory.

ANASTASIA: I know. I read it in my missal. You get years and years off for the rosary – and Novenas. I said a rosary for grandfather.

NONNA: Good. Good girl, darling.

ANASTASIA: Do you know what I'd like to do?

NONNA: What's that now?

ANASTASIA: Die on the way home from confession.

NONNA: What?

Scene Three ii

Wedding.

BRUNO (*off to* ALFREDO): Eh Fredo! Bimbo! Vieni qui.

ALFREDO (*shrugging apologetically to* LEONORA): Scusa.

ANASTASIA: Yes, die on the way home from confession. Get run over or something.

ALFREDO (*exiting*): I'll come back. I'll be back.

Scene Three iii

The beach.

ANASTASIA: Why not? I mean it! I always walk in the gutter and hope somebody's fallen asleep or's drunk or you know, mad, and runs me over . . . because then I'd be in a state of grace, wouldn't I? I'd go straight to heaven.

NONNA: No!

ANASTASIA: I would! Why wouldn't I?

NONNA: No, I mean – don't think things like that.

ANASTASIA: But what's the point of purgatory if you can avoid it? If grandfather could of?

NONNA *has confetti on her.*

ANASTASIA: Hey you've got sand all over you.

She starts to pick it off.

NONNA: Have I? Oh yes.

ANASTASIA: It's everywhere.

She picks it off.

NONNA: Thank you. Thank you, darling.

Scene Four

The past. Dublin 1963.
    JULIA-ALFREDO's *house. Dublin. Evening.* BRUNO *and* ALFREDO. BRUNO *in vest,* ALFREDO *in waistcoat and shirt sleeves, are playing scoba – Italian cards – on a small round table. A bottle of wine is half empty. It is late in the night.* BRUNO, *garrulous, tight, is scooping up another round's winnings – small change.*

BRUNO: You are the worst card player I ever met, Bimbo – but you don't help yourself. You always lay the wrong cards. Still – (*Dealing out a new hand.*) I make a few coppers – I don't complain. One more round? Eh?

ALFREDO (*tired*): And the next.

BRUNO: Well. What the hell? This is the best thing in life. No women, no babies, a game of cards and a few drinks. Fantastic!

They play for a while. JULIA's *head appears round the door.*

JULIA (*with warmth*): I'm going to bed, Alfredo. Do you want anything before I go?

ALFREDO (*with warmth*): No.

JULIA: Bruno?

BRUNO: Do I want anything? Can I have something rude?

JULIA (*sharp*): Sorry?

BRUNO: Nothing. I was joking.

JULIA: I see. (*To* ALFREDO:) Don't bolt the door . . . Peter said he'd be late. (*Comes over, kisses his head.*) 'Night.

ALFREDO: Goodnight, I'll be up later.

BRUNO: Buona notte.

They resume playing.

BRUNO: How old's Peter now?

ALFREDO: Nineteen . . . no twenty . . . twenty last January.

BRUNO: He's a good looking boy.

ALFREDO: Yes.

BRUNO: Not like his old man. (*Slaps* ALFREDO'*s back.*) Eh, come on! Cheer up. You're getting serious in your old age.

ALFREDO: Ha! Come on, it's your lay.

They play.

BRUNO: Is he still keen on this teacher nonsense?

ALFREDO: Yes – his mother wants him to carry on.

BRUNO (*sighs*): Si, si – Inglesi.

ALFREDO (*nods, rueful*): Si.

BRUNO: I know what I wanted to tell you.

ALFREDO: What's that?

BRUNO: Paulo – you know, my son in Milano – he's just graduated a doctor. What do you think of that! Fantastic. I'll tell you Alfredo, this life's a funny game. Twenty-five years old and I've never seen him (*Pours himself another drink.*) I mean . . . my own son.

ALFREDO: You don't have to tell me Bruno. I've got grandchildren. I've got two grandchildren. (*He's old, wistful.*) They send me letters. (*Nods to himself.*) I get letters from them.

BRUNO: When you think of it – that old puttana Maria producing me a doctor! – Do you remember all the fuss? . . . Papa – Whew! – I thought he was going to kill me he was so mad. And when he packed her off to Milano I never even wrote to her – not once – and then out of the blue – just like that – 'Dear Bruno, Paulo has graduated a doctor'. Fantastic. And her only a kitchen girl. I don't know . . . a funny business altogether. (*Pause.*) I remember that kitchen.

They play and they laugh.

BRUNO (*muses*): I wonder if she got fat. They all get fat, don't they? (*He begins to laugh – then* ALFREDO – *hysterically, remembering kitchen girls.*) Anita Falcinella! (*Laughs.*)

ALFREDO (*remembering kitchen girls*): Maria Bergamasco!

They laugh. Slapping each other. Coarse gestures. Then suddenly ALFREDO'*s face goes white – he begins to choke and rushes from the room.*

BRUNO (*anxious*): Eh Bimbo! Hey! Bimbo!

Scene Five

The past. Dublin, 1963.
  ALFREDO *is slumped in the lavatory. His face white. Blood beginning to seep from the corner of his mouth and from his nose.*

ALFREDO (*swallowing, coughing and snatches of breach punctuate all that follows*): I want a priest . . . Bruno. I want a priest . . . Quick. Madonna . . . Aiee Madonna.

BRUNO *hammers on the door.*

BRUNO: Alfredo! Let me in. Are you all right?

ALFREDO: Get a priest, quick, quick. Before it's too late.

BRUNO: Come on Bimbo, open up!

More hammering.

ALFREDO (*hoarse*): Stay out! Stay out! I want to confess. Get a priest. Please. Please.

BRUNO: Christ! (*Shouts:*) Julia! Julia!

. . . Look, Alfredo, hang on, can you? Just hang on. I'll be right back. (*Exits.*)

ALFREDO: Don't try and come in . . . it's disgusting.

He wipes his mouth and nose with his sleeve . . . a deep red stain on the cotton.

ALFREDO: Leonora, where are you?

NONNA (*off*): Yes?

JULIA appears outside the lavatory with BRUNO.

JULIA: Alfredo! What's going on? Are you all right?

ALFREDO: Julia? Is that you? Quick! Get a priest!

JULIA (*upset, worried*): What's he saying?

BRUNO: He wants a priest.

JULIA: He needs a doctor, not a priest! Can't you get him to let you in?

BRUNO: No. He said no.

JULIA (*to the door*): Darling. Open the door. Please.

BRUNO: He said no!

JULIA: Well, for Christ's sake, break it down!

BRUNO (*suddenly vehement*): No! He's my brother. Do as he says! Ring for a priest! (*To the door:*) We've sent for a priest, Bimbo. He'll be here straight away.

ALFREDO: Oi dio mamma . . . tell him to hurry . . . tell him thank you. (*Vague.*) Is he here? Is he here yet?

BRUNO (*lying*): Yes. He's arrived. He's here. Go ahead.

ALFREDO: Thank God. Bless me, Father, for I have sinned. It is (*Child's voice, tearful:*) O Father, I don't remember how long it is since I last made my confession and I accuse myself of these sins . . . I . . . (*Begins to mumble his confession.*)

Outside, JULIA returns.

JULIA: He was asleep. He'll be here in ten minutes. What's he doing? (*Tearful.*) What's he doing? (*To the door:*) Darling!

BRUNO (*distracted*): Sssh! He's making his confession. He's making his confession.

JULIA *slowly and methodically begins to thump on the door with her fist.*

ALFREDO (*continuing to confess*): . . . a pig's appetite . . . a pig in all things . . . forgive me . . . (*Hisses.*) weak like an animal . . . I beg absolution . . . all these years, no peace in my mind . . . forgive me . . . all of them abused . . . (*Coughs. Spasms.*) For these and for all my other sins which I cannot now remember, I beg pardon of God and penance and absolution of you, Father . . .

Pause.

ALFREDO: Bruno?

They stop thumping.

BRUNO: Yes. I'm here. I'm here. What? What is it?

ALFREDO: Peter. Look after him. Look after them all. Tell them all I'm sorry.

BRUNO: Yes. I'll tell them, Bimbo! Let me in, eh? Please! Bimbo! Bimbo!

They bang the door more and more violently. Finally BRUNO charges it down. ALFREDO is dead on the lavatory.

Scene Six

The present. England. Beach. NONNA and ANASTASIA are on the pier. Sitting in a shelter. ANASTASIA is fishing with a small handline. NONNA, distracted, weeping, is lost in her own thoughts. As ANASTASIA talks she experiments with her line.

ANASTASIA (*very bright*): My friend caught a crab on Saturday. A big one. I bet it was under here. I don't really want to catch one though. They're horrible. That's all you catch mostly when you go fishing off the pier. Crabs and things. I'm a bit frightened of them actually . . . Uncle Anthony pulls their legs off. Mam says I can go fishing with him next week, because you're not allowed to go on the pier with a proper fishing rod until you're 14, unless you've got somebody with you. But I can if he takes me. Then I can start catching all the fish for the shop. You get sharks sometimes, you know. Great big ones. I'd quite like to catch one of *those*. I don't know what bait you'd have to use though. I don't expect they'd eat worms. Paul Charlton says that sometimes when they catch sharks there are people living inside them. Still alive. Do you think that's true? He bet me that there were sixteen pounds in a stone once, and everybody knows that's not true. His dad takes him out fishing all night sometimes, and he doesn't have to go to sleep at all. They sit in the shelter with a blanket and fish over the side. All night. I'd like to do that one day. Don't expect I'd be allowed to though because I'm a girl. Dad can't take me. He's always working. Anyway, he can't even swim!

Scene Seven

The past, Dublin, 1963. JULIA *and* ALFREDO's *house.*

JULIA *is letting in a grown-up and married* GIOIA. *Both women are strained.*

GIOIA (*off. Unsure if this old woman is the dragon of history*): Mrs Jarrett?

JULIA (*off*): Come in.

GIOIA: I'm Gioia Powell. Alfredo Mare was my father.

JULIA: Yes. I remember you. You came to this house before. Many years ago.

GIOIA: Yes, I did.

JULIA: Would you like something to drink? Some tea? Did you come straight from the airport?

GIOIA: Yes. No tea, thank you. My mother's outside in the taxi. My sister's with her.

JULIA (*nodding*): Theresa.

GIOIA *doesn't reply.*

JULIA (*sighs*): I, put, what seemed appropriate, in a suitcase.

GIOIA: Right.

JULIA: You've grown to look more like him.

GIOIA (*closed*): Uhuh.

JULIA: Most things belong to his life here, of course, but there are things, his opera records, photographs of you girls, your mother, the families, the religious uh the religious items of his I packed for you to take. He's in the next room. I don't go in. I'm afraid it's not a custom I find . . . uh, I can't think of a word.

GIOIA: My uncle said they managed to give him the Last Sacrament.

JULIA: Your Uncle's in there with him now. And Peter.

GIOIA: Peter?

JULIA: Our son. He lives here.

GIOIA: We've arranged with the undertaker to take the coffin in the morning. Will 8.30 be convenient?

JULIA: Yes, that's quite convenient, thank you.

GIOIA: Anyway . . .

JULIA: Yes. Anyway. Is your mother coming in or what?

GIOIA (*embarrassed*): Would it be possible for you . . . I know that she . . . ?

JULIA: There would be no need for her to see me. I can sit in the kitchen.

GIOIA *nods. Pause.*

GIOIA: I expect the solicitors will contact you about his business effects and so on.

JULIA: He had no business effects here . . . are you talking about money? Is that what you're asking?

GIOIA: Really? That's not what we were led to believe.

JULIA: Oh? And what were you led to believe?

GIOIA: Frankly, I didn't anticipate having this kind of conversation over my father's body.

JULIA: We're not having a conversation over your father's body and it was your question.

GIOIA: And obviously one best left to solicitors.

JULIA: Gioia, your father – up until Christmas of last year – was a bingo caller. The hall was owned by Rank. When it closed so did his job. He retired. I work part-time in the Post Office. Those basically are the business effects.

GIOIA: I should fetch my mother. If you'll excuse me.

PETER *and* BRUNO *enter.* PETER *is about twenty years old.*

BRUNO (*to* GIOIA): Darling.

He embraces her miserably.

BRUNO: Your mother?

JULIA: Gioia is going to fetch her from the taxi. I wonder if you'd be good enough, Bruno, to take them in, to the, room? I'll be in the kitchen. Where will you be, Peter? This is Peter. Peter, this is Gioia.

PETER *nods.*

PETER (*to* JULIA): I'll come through with you. (*To* GIOIA:) We'd appreciate it if this wake . . . (*Sighs.*) After all, you do get to take him back with you. He lived in this house, you see, for more than twenty years. Anyway, we'd appreciate . . . as I said.

GIOIA: My sister wouldn't come in with me. Because she said if she saw your mother she wouldn't be responsible for her actions.

PETER: Did she! (*He could kill her.*)

JULIA (*to* PETER): Darling. Would you take my arm? (PETER *does so.*) Excuse us, won't you?

They exit with some dignity. BRUNO *looks embarrassed and confused.* GIOIA *is formidable.*

GIOIA: This house stinks of death.

BRUNO: It's not easy for anybody.

GIOIA: God judges us, Uncle, and He's not easy either. You can't erase a lifetime's hurt, simply shrug it off, for the sake of politeness. My mother's outside. She's had absolutely no life. Just given and given and given until a phone call comes in the night to say no more, it's gone, flushed down the lavatory. Come and collect the husk. And if that's hard on this house I'm very sorry.

BRUNO: Gioia . . .

GIOIA: I'll go and fetch mamma. She can't speak, probably. Theresa's with her. We'll all cry. We start each other off. If the noise is indiscreet, you must apologise for us. We have never had the luxury of good manners.

BRUNO (*softly, trying to soothe her*): Hey . . .

GIOIA: Why did you never say there was a son?

GIOIA *wants him to deny it.* BRUNO *shrugs.*

GIOIA: Oh, your family! My grandfather! Closed us off. Like turning off a tap. Not just money – though that smarts you know, all those years to see the gold on you everywhere – in your mouths, on your hands – and my mother scrabbling . . . no, it's the silence that rankles, the absolute silence. Was he really a bingo caller?

BRUNO (*sighs*): Your father was never much . . . business was never his . . . (*Trails off.*)

GIOIA: Christ!

BRUNO: You're lucky to have so little to be ashamed of.

GIOIA: Meaning?

BRUNO: Meaning? (*Sighs.*) Nothing. I'm sad. And it makes me more sad we're saying these things to each other.

He tries to embrace her. She remains rigid.

BRUNO: Really . . . mostly people live the best lives they can, darling.

GIOIA: I'm sorry, I don't believe that.

BRUNO: Yes, I know.

GIOIA: I'll go to the car. They'll be cold.

BRUNO: Gioia, why did your mother have to come here?

GIOIA: Oh, probably because her husband died, I expect.

Cries of seagulls.

Scene Eight

Dublin. The kitchen.
JULIA-PETER. JULIA *sits in the same rocking chair occupied by* LEONORA *at the beginning of play.* PETER *stands looking out, comes back as if from a window watching* LEONORA *enter the house. He comes back to his mother, stands behind her, massaging her neck and shoulders.*

JULIA (*sighs*): What did she look like?

PETER: I don't know. Old.

JULIA: When she was younger she was beautiful.

PETER: He told me once she had no passion, or something. No imagination. That none of them did.

JULIA: Did he say that? To you?

PETER: Yes. And Uncle Bruno said she'd come from a long line of sour servants.

JULIA: I don't think that's very fair. Do you?

PETER: Don't know. His daughter seemed . . .

JULIA: What did she seem?

PETER: Oh, bitter. Hard. It's quite incredible they refuse to acknowledge how much he loved you, mother. I mean, Christ, what do they imagine? That he stayed away all this time to be miserable with you?

JULIA: Oh, Peter . . .

PETER *stops massaging.*

JULIA: No, don't stop. (*She clasps his hands.*) It's so soothing.

PETER: Why did you give them his gramophone records? I should have liked them.

JULIA: Surely not? You've never listened to them.

PETER: I did! Anyway, that's not the point. (*Helplessly.*) I am half-Italian, too, you know.

JULIA *is weeping. She nods.*

PETER: He loved that music. I've seen tears in his eyes listening to those songs.

JULIA: Oh yes.

PETER: I mean, why couldn't they just leave us alone? They're in there now, vulturing him, kissing his cold forehead. Hysterical Italian vultures. Do they know him? I mean, how do they know they've got the right corpse?

JULIA: Please, Peter . . . let's be quiet together, hmm? The two of us.

Quiet.

JULIA: Listen . . . that sound . . .

PETER: It's outside. Someone sweeping leaves.

JULIA: Yes. There are so many this year. Do you hear them in the night? Rustling?

PETER: Yes. I hear them.

JULIA: I stood at the window this morning and watched them flutter past like so many flocks of birds. Like rain. The most marvellous colours. Your father said he could not remember a more beautiful Autumn.

She takes his hands in hers and kisses them.

Scene Nine

The present. England. Beach.
NONNA *and* ANASTASIA *walking, paddling.*

NONNA: You see I always prayed that he would come back. For a few days even. Just to show him how different things could have been. And he would have. He did want to. I know that. But he died too soon. Sitting on the lavatory in November. Did you know that? He died on the lavatory. His brother was outside the door, but your grandfather wouldn't let him in. Not even the doctor. Then the priest came . . . He made his confession through the door. He died with the priest giving him absolution outside . . . Is it turning cold, do you think? The sun's gone in . . . Uncle Bruno told me that he'd died of a broken heart . . . Oh yes, all along . . . in his heart . . . he'd wanted to come back to me. I knew that. But do you know something? That Mrs Jarrett didn't even go to the funeral . . . not that I would have let her . . . she just sent me a long letter saying your grandfather had

promised her a fur coat that had been
his mother's and would I please send it
to her? I had the coat on when the letter
arrived . . . But because grandfather had
mentioned it in some way . . . in some
document or other . . . or something
. . . I don't know . . . anyway I had to
hand it over. I wanted to suffocate her
with it. She stole everything from me.
She took my husband . . . then she
wanted the coat off my back. I feel sorry
for her now, in a way. She had no one
to comfort her. Just a fur coat . . .
(*Almost a laugh.*) With the moth in it.

ANASTASIA: Is she dead now?

NONNA (*continues*): We brought him
back from Dublin and buried him in a
double grave with my place ready beside
him. That's why I feel so sorry for Mrs
Jarrett . . . old puttana that she was . . .
(*Triumphant.*) She had him for a few
years. But I'll be with him for eternity.
We'll lie there together . . . the two of
us . . . for eternity.

ANASTASIA: So grandfather didn't love
her then?

NONNA: You're not listening. Looking
forward to your breakfast? Yes, of course
you are . . . Yes, I think I will just try
and walk out there a bit. (*She leaves
ANASTASIA behind.*) The sea looks
so warm. I wanted to tell you something.
Sometimes . . . shall I tell you what I
think about? I want to wade in . . · just
wade right up to my waist. (*Does so.*)
Feel my skirts floating around me . . .
These early mornings, when it's cool and
fresh . . . Yes . . . In the early mornings,
wade in past my waist and keep walking
and walking. (*Does so.*) Feel the water
churning round me. Swallow me up. You
know . . . they say a drowning man sees
his whole life before him. Shall I tell
you, Alfredo? These walks . . . these
paddles . . . that's a little like drowning
. . . isn't it?

*She walks, determined, towards the
water.*

TWO PLANKS AND A PASSION

For Norman Staveley

Two Planks and A Passion was first performed at the Northcott Theatre, Exeter in 1983 in a production commissioned and directed by Stewart Trotter and designed by Tim Reed. It was subsequently revised and presented at the Greenwich Theatre, London in 1984. For the Northcott Theatre production, the cast was as follows:

EDWARD YOUNG, *Pinner's labourer*	Keith Bartlett
WILL BLUEFRONT, *Painter's labourer*	David Oakley
GEOFFREY LE KOLVE, *Master, Painter's Guild*	Ted Valentine
WALTER PAYNTER, *apprentice painter*	Sean Aita
FATHER HENRY MELTON,	
Pardoner and Chaplain to the Painter's Guild	Patrick Romer
THOMAS ZACHARY, *Painter's labourer*	Mike Burnside
SARAH ZACHARY,	
his wife and lady-in-waiting to the Le Kolves	Heather Williams
KATHRYN LE KOLVE, *wife of Geoffrey*	Rosalind March
RICHARD II, *King of England*	Mark Jax
ROBERT DE VERE, *Earl of Oxford*	Saul Reichlin
ANNE OF BOHEMIA, *Queen of England*	Amanda Orton
ALICE SELBY, *Mayoress of York*	Amanda Walker
WILLIAM SELBY, *Mayor of York, Merchant.*	Raymond Cross
JOLYF ABSOLOM, *Herod in Merchants' play*	David Oakley
ARCHBISHOP OF YORK	Mike Burnside
GOD THE FATHER	
ADAM, *a servant boy*	
and assorted GODS, CHRISTS, SOLDIERS *and* CROWD	

ACT ONE

Scene One

Bells for five. Late May. Early morning. York, 1392.
Outside the Pageant House. This is a sort of medieval garage and is located in York.
It houses the Pageant Wagon of the Painters' Guild, shared with the Pinners and Latterners.
These three crafts play the Crucifixion Play, the thirty-fifth in the Corpus Christi Cycle.
WILL BLUEFRONT and EDWARD YOUNG appear, each dragging a plank of wood.
During the scene they join the two planks into a cross by lashing the wood together with
rope.

EDWARD: Don't it set your heart humming?

WILL: What?

EDWARD: Doing this. Making the cross. Getting together. Saying the words.

WILL: Says my words every evening. Before I sleeps.

EDWARD: Do you! And I do!

WILL: 'Stead of prayers.

EDWARD: This is different though, eh? Every year I just have to see our wagon, have a dibble round the costumes, put on my helmet, pull out the planks and I get a little flutter going.

WILL (*grumpily*): I'm not starting before cakes and ale.

EDWARD: Well, I doubt we'll get breakfast this year, Will. Everything's cut back, innit? I heard speak of another penny wanted from us for the play.

WILL: Who says? I'm not giving another penny. Anyway, we shouldn't have to pay if we're speaking in the pageant.

EDWARD: That's all very well for our Guild, but say you were doing the *Harrowing of Hell*? Fifty odd nipper in that all told. If they never paid up there'd be no play.

WILL: That's the Merchants' do anyway. What's a penny to them? They shit pennies.

EDWARD: I shit a sixpence once. It hurt. Picked it up at a fair and swallowed it for safe keeping.

WILL: They gets ham at the Merchants' rehearsals. And best beer.

EDWARD: Well . . . we gets the better play.

WILL: Now that's true. Where's the others then?

EDWARD: Oh, be along shortly, I expect.

WILL: I half thought to find Thomas pinned up on the cross from last year.

EDWARD: Not like Walter to be late, mind.

WILL: He'll be sent to search for the priest who'll no doubt be sleeping somewhere he shouldn't.

EDWARD: Shouldn't be rude about the parson, Will.

WILL: Well . . . If I puts my dick where I didn't ought it's a curse, Edward. If he do 'tis a blessing. Where's the fairness in that? So that's me and I'll not start before I'm given my breakfast.

EDWARD (*as a distraction*): Saw a dead heron this morning, me. That's bad luck. Means a famine.

WILL: Plague.

EDWARD: Aye. Or plague.

WILL: No – just plague.

EDWARD: Aye, it were a dead heron. Down by Ouse Bridge.

WILL: What do you do then? At night?

EDWARD: What do you mean?

WILL: When you're doing your words . . . who does my part?

EDWARD: Our missus. What about you?

WILL: No, I do it myself, me. I do all the parts.

EDWARD: The whole play?

WILL: Aye.

EDWARD: Oh.

WILL: I has to, Edward. I forget, see. Last year forgot my words, didn't I? Thought I'd get a fine.

EDWARD: Not forgot. Stumbled.

WILL: Forgot.

EDWARD: 'Tis easy done.

WILL: No. My brain's rusting. 'Nother year or two I'll be put out to pasture . . . I'll be off the wagon and down on the road pulling you boys round, station to station. Then you'll be first soldier.

EDWARD: Well.

WILL: No, if I give him to anyone it'll be to you. Unless your missus do him very well! How is she?

EDWARD: Oh, she's bonnie. Well, I say bonnie but you know she sold all her hair.

WILL: Never!

EDWARD: Aye. Had a new babe see. Needed the money.

WILL: I never knew. What's that? Nipper?

EDWARD: No. Little girl. Little lover, she is.

WILL (*sympathetically*): Lovely red hair she had an' all, your missus.

EDWARD: Aye.

WILL: Aye. If I pass him on to anyone will be to you, Edward.

EDWARD *lifts up the cross.*

EDWARD: Well, she's done then. Shall we have a go at it?

WILL: Aye.

EDWARD: With the moves?

WILL: No, can't do the moves, can we, missing Thomas. No, just the parts.

GEOFFREY LE KOLVE *and* WALTER *approach.*

GEOFFREY: How do, lads?

EDWARD:
WILL: 'Morning Mister.

WALTER: Will. Edward.

WILL: No Tom yet.

WALTER (*covering up*): He's here. He's with the parson.

GEOFFREY (*innocuously*): Have we had bells for five?

EDWARD: We have, sir.

WILL (*pointedly*): We've had bells for quarter past five.

GEOFFREY: Really? Well, the parson hears a confession yet but he'll be along shortly. Walter can get you going. (*Ominously.*) There are a change or two this year.

WILL: We're due breakfast, Mister.

GEOFFREY: Has that not come either?

WILL: No. Neither.

GEOFFREY: I'll see to it.

WILL: Please, Mister.

GEOFFREY: Completely forgot.

WILL: Mister: we heard speak of more pageant pence wanted.

GEOFFREY (*defensively*): I know. These plays is costing the Guilds a fortune. I know, lads. A penny's a lot. *I* can't spare a penny just so. Not like some: sitting on their arses on the dry land while a ship sails making them a fortune. No, I'm opposed to more pageant pence, me. There's talk of sharing our play with the Masons.

WILL (*outraged*): Never!

EDWARD (*outraged*): What!

GEOFFREY: Oh aye! And I'm the one who's talking! Aye! These pageants is nothing but a pestilence in my opinion. An excuse for time off and clowning about.

WILL (*offended*): *Five* morning we rehearse, Mister. And that off our wage.

GEOFFREY: We has more feast days in this country than work days.

WALTER (*conciliatorily*): We should get going lads. There's new words for us all.

GEOFFREY: No use moaning to me, Will. I've got cakes and ale to dole out. I've got pullers to pay. I've got lights to buy. I've got a mask to leaf in gold. How much is that costing? (*He looks to* WALTER.)

EDWARD: We all contribute.

GEOFFREY: To me, see: I'm no reveller . . . these days is just Christ done mischief to above the wagon and more mischief done underneath. Half the watchers pissed or sleeping or feeling each other. There's more thought of whoring than of God.

WALTER (*shrewdly*): Last year it were reckoned our pageant was finest played.

GEOFFREY (*egotistically*): Oh aye. I know that. It were reckoned we were a bull among bullocks!

WILL (*bull*): We were.

GEOFFREY: I know that. I know that. But we has to save money, Walter. It is as Will says, many things come before a play.

WILL (*wounded again*): Never said that! 'Tis our play and we'll not lose it for the sake of a penny.

GEOFFREY: Then be careful not to lose it for the sake of complaining. (*Sternly.*) Now I wants reckoning of savings to take back to the Guild, Walter.

WALTER: Aye, Mister.

GEOFFREY: Else these plays is cancelled. That's my mind spoke. So. And bid the priest come see me sharpish. (*He makes to exit.*) 'Morning, lads.

ALL: 'Morning, Mister.

GEOFFREY *exits.*

WILL (*as soon as* GEOFFREY *is out of earshot*): 'I can't spare a penny just so!' His bed cost twenty pound!

EDWARD: You shouldn't grumble so, Will. Makes matters worse.

WILL: Why? Because he threatens us? He can't cut our play. The sky would fall on his head. What would they do, eh? Miss out the crucifixion? Ach!

WALTER: No, they'd give it to the Merchants.

WILL: Every year we hear the same story; 'tis to keep our hands tied behind us.

EDWARD: One minute you moan about more money; the next about less.

WILL: Aye, I do! 'Tis a duty to play the play. And even if God would forgive us the town would not.

WALTER: An' I tell you, the Merchants would take our pageant and no one would protest, except us.

WILL: Except us. US would be sufficient! Don't give us the master's view, Mister Apprentice. We know it.

EDWARD: Leave off, Will.

WILL: Well.

EDWARD: Thing is, Walter, me and Will and the others . . . Tom . . . we done this pageant years, see. Just the thought of playing her warms cold fingers in January . . . beats the heart come Spring. It's our occasion, in' it?

WALTER (*hurt*): I love the play no less than you do.

EDWARD: Course you do.

WILL (*knowing this, but still grumpy*): What changes anyway?

WALTER: They've cut the end business with the purple cloak.

WILL: And why's that?

WALTER: Too long. Been complaints from the council about running time. It's reckoned that all forty-eight plays got to be seen within the day, including the Mass.

EDWARD: Not possible.

WALTER: I know it, Edward, but just the same we cut some. Besides, then we pay less for lights – if we're shorter . . . and if you lose the dividing-up of the cloak that's a purple cloth saved.

WILL: Ach! Saved! We know what's saved, nipper. 'Tis what's lost is the bugger. These pageant masters would be masters of no pageant at all left up to them. Yet they're never so happy while they can hoof ahead of us, all plush with our banner. Great galleybagging gang.

EDWARD: Don't yoppel on so, Will.

WALTER: They also want less of the soldiers early on.

WILL: Do they! And what about less Mary?

WALTER: No. There's less Mary already.

WILL (*caustically*): Oh aye! And not because you're groomed for pageant master. We can all clot, Mister. You clot with that lot, please yourself. We'll all clot together.

WALTER: I would do less Mary, Will. I'd do *no* Mary and something else, given the chance. I do have a beard now. (*He feels it.*) Some. And I'm betrothed. I long to act in hose and not in petticoat. But I don't choose that neither. I play the Virgin and you play less soldier. There: view the changes.

WILL: You know I don't know letters. None of us do.

EDWARD: I know some. I know E for Edward and Y for Young and P for Pinner and some others.

WILL: I'm talking about reading, Edward, and you can't. Nor can any of us saving Mr Walter here.

WALTER: I'll learn you your parts and we'll do well.

EDWARD: That's kind, Walter.

WALTER: You making blood yet, Will?

WILL: I done it a week ago.

EDWARD: Looks marvellous real. You'd think he'd bled himself. And I made new pins.

WALTER: This year our pageant's having a fresh face for Christ. I'm making him. A quarter ounce of silver in it.

EDWARD: I could eat off that whole winter. Longer.

WILL: Still. It's the Lord's face. Should be special.

WALTER: Amen.

EDWARD: Amen.

WALTER: So. We're starting. You each had five speeches before Christ had his.

WILL (*showing all his fingers*): Then ten and I call on company to lift the cross.

WALTER: No, hold up, Will. Now Thomas speaks once only for Christ and that at the end. So where he spoke first he now says nothing and you continue but lose your speech before he spoke and after. You with me?

EDWARD: So, we says five and then straight away ten and then company?

WALTER: No, you says four and then nine and then company.

WILL (*grumpily*): 'Tis irregular now though, ain't it? 'Cause I used to have one hand's worth beforehand and two hands' worth after.

EDWARD: Always were irregular, 'cause I always used to say four lines then you would say two lines and . . .

WILL: And different counts. (*Muttering.*) It's a bugger if you ask me. 'Tis buggered up for no good reason.

EDWARD: Oh, I think 'tis a nice touch to have the Christ dumb until the end.

WILL: Edward, you'd thank a bugger for bashing you!

WALTER (*delicately*): Do get more complex later, Edward, to tell you the truth.

EDWARD (*maudlin*): Oh.

WILL (*grumpily*): Aye: Bloody oh!

FATHER HENRY MELTON, THE CHAPLAIN *and* PRODUCER, *enters with* THOMAS.

FATHER MELTON: Have I missed the breakfast?

WALTER: No Father, it comes yet.

FATHER MELTON: 'Tis a real penance the Lord sent me: hunger. I hunger through the night like no other man I know.

WILL (*close*): And what was you up to Thomas: Confessing?

THOMAS: No, I . . . no, couldn't wake up.

WILL: Some of us have been here half an hour. But then we aint' got a new wife in our cots.

WALTER: We begun, Father, we're learning changes.

FATHER MELTON: Splendid. I've made alterations lads, to improve the speeches. And 'tis also shorter. If a thing is worth talking about for ten minutes 'tis better said in one. And in plain words, in English.

WALTER: I've touched on the differences, Father.

FATHER MELTON: Aye. 'Tis the picture speaks, in my view. Not the words. Oh yes. So I'm sad about losing the cloth, me, and the dice. The masters tell me 'tis an expense and not necessary. (*He shrugs.*) And Walter, do you still speak for the Virgin? You have increasingly a beard.

WALTER: I do, Father, but I'll scrape it shortly.

FATHER MELTON: Were it to me, I'd have a girl say it, no offence. A beautiful girl were chosen for the deed, a beautiful girl should say it. Still, the masters would cut the pageant and the Archbishop would stop it altogether. So, Walter, you're preferred to nothing.

WALTER: Thank you, Father.

FATHER MELTON: See, left to me I'd never show Christ wounded. No, I'd take a strapping lad and paint his whole flesh gold, not just the face alone, and have him golden, transcendent on the tree in majesty. So come the great speech, he'd slip the nails and rope and stand arms stretched in blessing, not in pain. (*Acting his fantasy.*) Oh yes . . . But the taste is for mumbling and hurt and violence and cruelty.

THOMAS *couldn't be less appropriate for this vision. He's middle-aged and fat.*

EDWARD: But surely, Pastor, if we show not Christ's suffering, how can we teach men to sorrow at it and seek forgiveness?

FATHER MELTON: Ach. The world is swollen with suffering and sorrow. I've seen enough of it. Still, let's begin and do the moves alone. All the bashing and the bother. Get yourself on the tree now, Tom. I want to show the soldiers the new moves.

EDWARD: How do, Thomas?

EDWARD *helps* THOMAS *to the cross.*

THOMAS (*cautiously*): Oh. Fair.

EDWARD (*to* WILL): Looks a bit wan, don't he, Will?

WILL (*mischievously*): I said, 'tis that new young wife of his: tiring him out. Looks older'n me now.

THOMAS: I *am* older'n you.

WILL: Aye, but you never looked it before. This year you do. I bet our young apprentice over there, him with his bumfluff, I bet he regrets giving her up for his big ideas.

WALTER *comes across to help* TOM *get on the cross.*

WALTER: What's this?

WILL: No, I'm just saying: new moves and all now, is it?

The three men rope THOMAS *to the cross which is propped up so as to keep* THOMAS *visible. During this:*

WILL: I can remember when there were four soldiers, me. Each year they takes something away. Soon they'll have the Christ crucifying hisself and no soldiers at all.

WALTER (*having had enough of* WILL): You see one bird, it's a flock, ain't it Will?

WILL: Maybe. What do one spot of rain signal to you? Signal a thousand to me. All this to-do. 'Tis bad token. 'Tis bees out of a hole.

EDWARD: Here comes our breakfast, lads.

FATHER MELTON: Thank the Lord for that.

SARAH ZACHARY, THOMAS's *wife, waiting-woman for the Le Kolves and one-time sweetheart of* WALTER, *enters. She's loaded up with the cakes (bread-cakes) and beer.*
    FATHER MELTON *walks towards* SARAH.

How do, Sarah? Do you bring our beer? Bless you. Jump down then Thomas and eat.

SARAH: How do, lads. Is it hungry work crucifying?

WILL: 'Tis mistress. Particular we eat an hour after we should.

SARAH (*sweetly, to her husband*): Can I help you, husband?

THOMAS (*half-crucified but cheerful*): No. I manage. Do you, with that weight? (*Meaning the jug of beer, etc.*)

SARAH: Aye.

    SARAH *moves across to* WALTER *as the group settles down to breakfast and* THOMAS *disentangles himself from the cross.*

SARAH: Walter.

WALTER: Sarah.

SARAH: And how is it with you, sir?

WALTER: I'm well, mistress. An' you?

SARAH: Aye.

WALTER: Fair enough.

SARAH: We heard you was betrothed then.

WALTER: Aye.

SARAH: Eleanor dell Brigg. That's a good match for you, Walter.

WALTER: Aye. They say so.

SARAH: I'm glad then. And you've got a little beard.

WALTER: Aye. A little.

WILL (*facetiously*): Going to rub off that fluff, make a paint brush, eh Walter?

SARAH (*to* WALTER): I has to measure you for your new dress.

WALTER (*uncomfortably*): Not drinking, Thomas?

THOMAS: Will do.

EDWARD: You are queer quiet, Thomas.

THOMAS (*mindful of* SARAH *and* WALTER): Ngh.

EDWARD: You sickening?

THOMAS: No.

WILL: Done hisself an injury on the planks.

WALTER: Have some cakes.

WILL: I heard say at Beverley last year, from John Lunn, that their Christ on the Pinners' pageant got hisself crucified real. Hung him up like a hare they did. He couldn't get his breath. They thought he were pretending but he weren't. Couldn't tell, see, under his mask.

EDWARD: Poor nipper.

WILL: Oh aye, and at Coventry they didn't care much for their boy and thumped in the nails right through his hands.

THOMAS: Never!

WILL: Ah! So you *have* still got your tongue.

THOMAS: They never did!

WILL: So 'tis said.

THOMAS: Did they, Parson?

FATHER MELTON: Take no notice, Thomas.

THOMAS: I bet they never.

WALTER: Come and eat, Thomas.

SARAH: Thomas Zachary, you're an old donkey if you listen to this gang. Dip your nose in the jug, lovely, and shut up.

> THOMAS *sulks across.*
> KATHRYN LE KOLVE *appears.*

(*Jumping up.*) Mistress!

KATHRYN: How do.

> The MEN *jump up.*

No. Don't stand on ceremony, lads. I needs a word apart with the priest. 'Morning Walter. How goes the rehearsal?

WALTER (*wearily*): Very punctuated, madam.

KATHRYN: How's that?

WALTER: As yet it has few starts and many stops.

KATHRYN: Aye well: proceed. Proceed. Can they proceed, Parson?

FATHER MELTON: I fear they waits on me, madam.

KATHRYN: Then come apart, quick. (*She pulls the priest aside.*)

FATHER MELTON (*as KATHRYN pulls him away*): Point out the changes, Walter.

> There are frustrated looks from the actors at a further hiatus. They pack up their breakfast during what follows:

KATHRYN (*unburdening her news immediately*): Henry, I heard the Earl of Oxford came last night to stop at the Mayor's house.

FATHER MELTON: Oxford? Impossible. He's exiled.

KATHRYN: Not by the King. He says the King comes here. He says the King will be here this morning. And Queen. And retinue.

FATHER MELTON: Why?

KATHRYN: The King is sullen with London, is the word.

FATHER MELTON: His Majesty is a man of culture. Why should he come here? No, 'tis idle this rumour. (*Conscious of the others.*) Be with you directly, lads.

KATHRYN (*undeterred*): And what if the King came to be with the Earl? 'Tis said that when Oxford were at court he could make Richard see black as white and white as black.

FATHER MELTON (*excited*): Would it were true. Would spice the town.

KATHRYN: I'm off to spice myself.

FATHER MELTON: My God, Kathryn. I hope he stop for the pageant and like mine. I'd give my splinter from the true cross for some gold paint and good cloth and even half good players. I must plead with your husband for more money not less. Oh Christ! The King! The King! He might bring me to court and I could give up scratching here.

KATHRYN (*hurt*): Oh?

FATHER MELTON: No I didn't mean. I meant . . .

KATHRYN: What?

FATHER MELTON: I just meant good. You know: exciting.

WALTER: Should we do the moves, Parson?

FATHER MELTON: Aye, do the moves.

Bells ring severally and noisily.

THOMAS:
EDWARD: Yow!

EDWARD: What's this!

All react.

WILL: Christ's blood! Them jangle! What's up, then?

EDWARD: Told you, Will. That heron! 'Tis bad luck, I bet! 'Tis a famine!

WALTER: What bells are these, Parson?

FATHER MELTON: What bells? They're all the bells!

WALTER: Aye, but what do they signify?

FATHER MELTON: I don't know, boy.

KATHRYN (*delighted*): I think it may be the King coming!

ALL: The King!

KATHRYN: Aye.

WILL (*shouting at the bells*): Why?

EDWARD: Never heard so many bells.

WILL: All right we heard!

GEOFFREY *runs in, yelling over the tumult.*

GEOFFREY (*shouting*): The King comes! The King comes!

The bells stop.
(*Still shouting.*) The King comes!

KATHRYN: Aye, husband, they know.

GEOFFREY: How do they know?

KATHRYN: I told them.

GEOFFREY: How do you know, madam?

KATHRYN (*dissembling*): Oh. (*Meaning, never you mind.*)

GEOFFREY (*deflated*): Don't just gawp, nippers. There's no rehearsal now. We're out at the gates to greet the Royal Party. Get to, Walter. The Mayor's craft is half way there.

KATHRYN: They can't go dressed so.

GEOFFREY: No. You can't go dressed so. Go and change into Sunday outfit and fetch our banner.

WALTER *and* WILL *exit.*

Shift that cross, Thomas, Edward. Don't dawdle! You're all dawdling! Come on, come on! 'Tis a race not a funeral! Let's meet directly by Mickelgate.

KATHRYN: Sarah, go back to the house and pull out my maroon gown. It needs spicing.

FATHER MELTON (*excited*): I'll hurry, too. I've a sword to buckle on and 'tis a chance to wear my new cross from Venice. I'll see you both at Mickelgate.

FATHER MELTON *exits.*

GEOFFREY (*sourly*): That priest is a penance.

KATHRYN: He's nothing of the sort. He can read. And he forgives me. 'Tis two things *you* can't do. At least.

GEOFFREY: Ach! And what do this King want now? Christ! 'Tis one trial after another. And how is it, woman, you know the business of the town before I do?

KATHRYN: I listens, sir. You spend so much time talking. If you want to know, I heard the King is in sulk with London.

GEOFFREY: How in sulk?

KATHRYN: For respecting not His Majesty.

GEOFFREY: Ah! 'Tis a money thing then.

KATHRYN: Some others say the King love this Oxford more than his wife.

GEOFFREY: Woman, most men love most men more than their wife.

KATHRYN: Oh!

GEOFFREY: Not me. I kiss your fingers, madam, and if your foot came more often to my bed I would kiss that also.

KATHRYN: I hate your bed. It's straw.

GEOFFREY: Then let me come to yours.

KATHRYN: With my maid at the foot of it? 'Tis not seemly.

GEOFFREY: For my part I would throw out the maid.

KATHRYN: For my part you should throw out the bed, sir, and find a new one more suitable. That's the remedy.

GEOFFREY: Madam, I spent twenty pounds on your bed because of your horror of the straw one. Now I has the straw one.

KATHRYN: Aye, husband. That's true.

GEOFFREY: Well . . . ach, Christ's blood!

KATHRYN: Where do we greet the King, sir?

GEOFFREY: By Ouse Bridge.

KATHRYN: Oh no! Not me. That bridge stinks and I'll not sniff it.

GEOFFREY: It does not stink.

KATHRYN: You have no nose, husband, how would you know? If you would buy me parfum I could travel more. I could smell myself and not the foul air. I will not walk neither. You may be happy to greet a King with skirts beshitted. I am not. No, I'll not stand by Ouse Bridge, why should we? Where is the Mayor and his monkey meeting the Royal Party?

GEOFFREY: City Gates.

KATHRYN: Then that's where we'll go. Don't settle for second best, husband. It's a bed you make for yourself. 'Tis unattractive. Run ahead now, and arrange horses and a better view. (*Thinking.*) If a King comes, profit comes in his train. Run!

GEOFFREY *huffs.*

But not sweatily, sir!

GEOFFREY: Ach.

GEOFFREY *exits unhappily. Then* KATHRYN *exits, happily.*

Scene Two

The Mayor's house.
This is the bedroom or upper storey.
In the room RICHARD II, *his Queen,* ANNE OF BOHEMIA, *and the exiled Earl,*
ROBERT DE VERE *of Oxford, are reunited.* RICHARD *is embracing* OXFORD.

RICHARD: Robert!

OXFORD: Richard! Anne! Marvellous.

ANNE (*concerned*): Robert, you're grey.

OXFORD (*shrugging*): Dust. (*Concerned.*) You're thin.

ANNE (*tightly*): I don't think so.

RICHARD: When did you come? Yesterday?

OXFORD: Aye. Last evening.

ANNE: Let's not go down. Let's stay up here and talk.

RICHARD: There's a feast done for us.

ANNE (*mischievously*): Say I sicken.

OXFORD: Oh do, please, Majesty. The people here will speak French and cannot. I
    want to speak English. I would not care if I never heard a *bonjour* or a *bonsoir* before
    purgatory. Tell me of London.

RICHARD: No.

ANNE: He hates London now, Robert. Without you. Without friends. Without
    money.

OXFORD: Is it bad?

RICHARD: Worse. The city vomits merchants and lawyers. The court conspires.
    Gloucester and Bolingbroke torment me. London's piss drowns me.

ANNE (*sadly*): I cannot conceive there, Robert. I lost two babies since we last spoke.

RICHARD: The Parliament would speak my words for me. They call me weak because
    I love not warmongering and the endless bloodying.

OXFORD: And because you once loved Oxford.

RICHARD: Still do, friend.

OXFORD: Oh, London still sounds like heaven after Calais and Bordeaux and those
    puddles of nowhere, Sire. Not a sun but I thought of you, not a laugh but I heard
    yours, not a game but I saw you play it, not a pageant but I remembered your
    hurrah.

RICHARD: No laughs now, Robert, nor games. London is loveless.

OXFORD: Then it is you who is London in my heart and now London is in York with
    Oxford.

ANNE: And Bohemia.

OXFORD: And Bohemia!

RICHARD: I kicked out the Mayor at home, Robert, and his crew, and they can linger
    on my pleasure.

OXFORD: Bravo.

RICHARD: It were never meant for tradesmen to govern. It is against God that a King should be worked from below.

OXFORD: But what do you hope for here?

ANNE: Rest.

RICHARD: Give them a few weeks, the fat cats will purr for me again. Meanwhile, we three can live a little out of time.

ANNE: We might move the court here if it pleases us.

OXFORD: I only fear that this place is more of the same. The Mayor here is so full of Mayor he cannot squeeze into his gown an inch of wit.

RICHARD: He bowed and scraped an hour outside the gates until I fell asleep on his speech. We waded here, Robert. Half the town oozing on us.

OXFORD: And the Mayoress is inflated. Like a pig's bladder for football. She knows nothing and insists on revealing it.

ANNE: This is a fine bed.

RICHARD: Anne judges each new place by its bed.

ANNE: I do. This bed is a better bed than ours, Richard.

OXFORD: Ask them for it. They can't refuse.

RICHARD: I might.

OXFORD: Get all their beds away from them. They'd hate you for it.

RICHARD: Is that good?

OXFORD: It will flatter them you want their beds. Each will out-peacock the other until they realize that to show off so they must lose what they most prize: the thing. 'Tis a people of thing, these guildsmen.

ANNE: What 'thing'?

OXFORD: A 'thing'. Any 'thing'. Beds, bolsters, pisspots, conduits, baubs, trinkets, hangings . . . anything. What breeding they lack inside they disguise in this weight of thing. They even die now and have these things buried with them.

RICHARD: You've not changed, Robert.

OXFORD: Demand these things. That what they own is coveted is essential to their design . . . that a King wants them is marvellous. They'll bestow them on you flushed with conceit and next flushed with anxiety. They know the worth of each thing down to the last farthing and will cost out their generosity tear by tear.

RICHARD: This polemic cost you your land, your fortune and London's favour.

OXFORD: Good riddance then, eh?

ANNE: And you have one rule for your friends and another for the world.

OXFORD: Who has not? I hate the pig with power, the donkey with degree. I hate books unread and songs unheard and glass unviewed and all beauty wasted. And I talk too much.

ANNE: You do, and I love it.

RICHARD: And I do.

ANNE: I'll have the bed. The colour suits me. I think I'll lie down on it, too. Come boys and cosset me. (*They do.*) Ah, that's nice.

RICHARD: Do you know this woman has been sick, Oxford?

OXFORD: How sick?

RICHARD: She swoons on me and fevers on me and coughs and chokes and spasms on me. No thought of my peace. (*Gently.*) Is that not so, madam?

ANNE: I'm inconsiderate.

RICHARD: January she even feigned death to grieve me. (*He clasps* ANNE's *hand.*)

OXFORD (*clasping* ANNE's *other hand.*) Hussy.

ANNE: I know.

OXFORD (*gently*): Your hands are so cold.

RICHARD: And dead babes she hands me, just so.

OXFORD: Wicked. Come on, let me warm your hands, madam.

ANNE (*sad*): The babies: 'tis too many eyes on me, Robert, none friendly.

OXFORD: Then we will make of this a season of sport to cure us all.

RICHARD: Amen.

ANNE: To mischief!

OXFORD: To mischief!

RICHARD: To mischief!

OXFORD (*only half believing what he says*): And surely come the autumn: London, starved of majesty, will embrace you.

ANNE: And we can bring you back in our train.

OXFORD: I like this scheme.

RICHARD: Robert, what of the play here? How is it?

OXFORD: Good, I hear.

RICHARD: If it rivals Coventry 'tis the one thing the country does to out-art London.

ANNE: Richard, show him your wipe.

OXFORD: What's this?

RICHARD: My wipe!

OXFORD: I'm lost.

RICHARD *produces a large handkerchief and blows his nose.*

Ha!

RICHARD *hands it to* ANNE *who blows hers.*

RICHARD: Robert . . .

ROBERT *blows his nose. He laughs.*

It saves the sleeve, eh?

They grin hugely.

OXFORD: Whose invitation is this?

ANNE: Richard's.

OXFORD: 'Tis very strange.

RICHARD: How strange! 'Tis very wondrous! I have many and use them variously: one for the nose; one for the arse; one for the brow.

ANNE: An' he mix them up.

OXFORD: True. 'Tis very wondrous.

RICHARD: Here, (*He fishes around and produces half a dozen handkerchiefs.*) try them.

ANNE: The Parliament call him woman for this hygiene.

OXFORD: I call them shit flies for theirs!

RICHARD: To women then!

OXFORD: And away with shit flies.

ANNE: Away with them!

Scene Three

The Mayor's house. A room below.
  The Mayor and Mayoress wait to eat and wonder how you tell a King he's late for dinner.

ALICE: What transpires up there, husband?

WILLIAM: I don't know.

ALICE: They don't have their servants in with them. That's unnatural.

ALICE: How unnatural?

WILLIAM: Well, 'tis not done, is it?

ALICE: What the King do becomes what's done, madam.

  ALICE *whispers confidential rumours about* OXFORD's *exploits.*

  Why whisper, wife, when we're alone?

ALICE: Such things should not be shouted. (*She whispers some more.*)

WILLIAM: Well, I don't know, do I? They come from London and have different customs.

ALICE: Should we learn them, then?

WILLIAM: I don't know. What I do know is I'm hungered and my belly rumbles and churns and can sniff the table.

ALICE: We can't eat until they come down. The Queen has bathed herself. And the King. Is that the fashion too? To come in from outdoors and wash the body?

WILLIAM: I *don't* know!

ALICE: I'm certain the physic would say it risks sickness . . . but if it be the fashion we should do it, husband, and encourage the town.

WILLIAM: Woman, I am already the laughing stock with all this hygiene law you make me champion.

ALICE: 'Tis the smell of pig particular offends me.

WILLIAM: Never used to.

ALICE: And Kathryn Le Kolve told she read in a book that in Italy they have a law against *any* slops in the street.

WILLIAM: Madam . . . think for one second, pray . . . if you cannot pour out the slops onto the street, what do you do with it?

  ALICE *can't think of an answer to this argument.*

ALICE: Well she said the Italians have a law against it.

WILLIAM (*sulky*): I'll not strip my clothes every day; it's a business.

ALICE: Aye. Well. His Majesty have a cloth, too. He use it most mysteriously. Wiping. Hm. I suppose I could have made some up.

WILLIAM: Madam . . . eight shillings of mutton and venison and capon rot on our table while we prattle on about the fashion of arses – whether we should poke them or wash them or wipe them. For me I want food in my gut so as to do with my arse what God made it for and I will continue to slop out its product until God or you show me a way of magically vanishing it.

ALICE (*placating*): William . . .

WILLIAM: What?

ALICE *strokes* WILLIAM.

Stop it.

ALICE: Willum . . . Willum . . .

WILLIAM: Whatee?

ALICE: We has a King and Queen in our house, husband.

WILLIAM: I know.

ALICE: The town be green.

WILLIAM: I know.

ALICE: So green – Kathy Le Kolve will sicken with greenness.

WILLIAM: And her husband.

ALICE: They'll be so green they dare not walk the pastures less a cow graze on them.

WILLIAM (*proudly*): Always stayed before in the Castle or the Abbey. Always.

ALICE: Get this noted in the record book then; tonight a King and Queen sleep in the bed of William and Alice Selby.

WILLIAM: Our bed?

ALICE: Where else?

WILLIAM: Where do we sleep? In the front?

ALICE: No, the Earl must sleep there.

WILLIAM: Where then?

ALICE: I'm to my mother's house and you down with your sons.

WILLIAM: With the dogs and the rabble?!

ALICE: You'll not die of it. Oh, and we must buy music, too. This King loves music.

WILLIAM: Why buy? Can't we invite someone over?

ALICE: That's no use. He must have proper minstrels. Leave it with me.

WILLIAM: Ach! It don't feel good all this cost.

ALICE: Listen, husband, you have twenty cases at law.

WILLIAM: Twenty-four.

ALICE: Well then, get the King's favour and think on it. Think, too, on *Sir* William Selby.

WILLIAM: Sir William. Sir Will.

ALICE: Lady Alice.

WILLIAM: My Lady.

ALICE: My Lord.

WILLIAM: What – my Lady?

ALICE: Oh. (*Mock sigh.*) Nothing, my Lord.

They dance gleefully. Then eventually WILLIAM *pulls up.*

WILLIAM: By Christ that flesh smells good.

ALICE: I know. It do. Let's go up, eh?

Scene Four

The Mayor's house. The bedroom.
ANNE, RICHARD *and* OXFORD *are sprawled on the bed.*

WILLIAM (*off*): Majesty? Majesties?

OXFORD: 'Tis the dog after his dinner.

WILLIAM (*off*): Majesties . . .

RICHARD: Should we stay a-bed and scandalize them?

OXFORD: Aye. Let's.

WILLIAM (*off*): Majesties.

ALICE (*off*): His Worship the Mayor and Lady Mayoress approach the Royal Salon.

OXFORD (*mock impressed*): Salon!

RICHARD: *Entrez.*

RICHARD *and* ALICE *enter.*

WILLIAM: We *entrez maintenant*, Your Most Shining Radiance.

ALICE: Forgive this *petite* intrusion.

RICHARD: *Nous sommes ici, madame. Au lit.*

ALICE *tries not to look surprised.*

ALICE: Pardon?

RICHARD (*very swiftly*): *Parce que vous vous dandinez en parlant le francais, j'ai pensé, faussement, que vous compreniez la langue et désiriez la parler avec nous.*

ALICE (*lost*): Um . . . pardon?

WILLIAM (*hungry and very lost*): The thing is, my Lord, the feast cools and the flies visit the table before we do.

ANNE: Ugh!

RICHARD: My wife sickens, Mayor, and would eat in our 'salon'.

WILLIAM: Uh . . .

ALICE: Of course, Your Majestic . . . · uh . . . Majesty.

RICHARD: What is the fare?

ALICE: Capons . . . mutton . . . venison . . . small bird, sturgeon, pike.

ANNE: 'Tis excessive, madam.

ALICE: Uh . . .

WILLIAM: 'Tis in your honour, Your Shining Beacons.

ANNE: Do you not have poor in the town?

ALICE: We do, ma'am.

ANNE: Good, then they should taste of this feast, in our honour. Say the King and his Queen wish to thank the citizens for their generous hospitality. That is our pleasure.

WILLIAM (*distraught*): Distribute it to the poor, glorious Lady?

ANNE: Aye. It should go out to the streets this minute. In truth the stench of it poisons my nostrils somewhat. (*Innocently.*) Have you ate?

WILLIAM: No, no, we waited on you, sweet Queen.

ANNE: Shame. Still, fasting's good for choler.

WILLIAM: Does our feast not please you, glorious Majesty?

ANNE: Oh yes, it do. Most sincere.

OXFORD: What pleases the Queen more, sir, is this bed.

ANNE: Marvellous bed.

OXFORD: And the King like it.

RICHARD: Very fine bed.

ANNE (*to* RICHARD): I'd like the bed, sir. Might I not have one like it?

RICHARD: 'Tis not mine to give, Lady. Though were it I'd delight in bestowing it on you.

WILLIAM (*miserably*): 'Tis mine, madam, now 'tis yours.

ANNE: No. Surely not!

ALICE: Oh yes, gracious Sovereign, 'tis our joy to gift it.

ANNE: Then I'm happy now. And like this place which hitherto I liked not much.

RICHARD (*explaining*): The Queen find too much air in here.

ANNE: Oh? Do I?

RICHARD: You do, madam.

ANNE: I do.

ALICE: One could draw the canopy, sire, and shelter from any draught. 'Tis what I do.

RICHARD: How, mistress?

ALICE: Like so. (*Struggling with the bed canopy.*) Help, William.

WILLIAM: Aye. Beg pardon.

WILLIAM *and* ALICE *draw the curtains half round the bed.*

RICHARD: Do they not surround us, then?

WILLIAM: Can do. Can do.

RICHARD: Then do. Then do.

WILLIAM *and* ALICE *curtain off the bed by means of the canopy. The* King, Queen *and* OXFORD *are now completely hidden.* WILLIAM *and* ALICE *exchange glances. They don't know what to do next. There's a pause. Then William coughs.*

WILLIAM: Majesty?

RICHARD: Aye? What is it?

WILLIAM: Do you want else?

RICHARD: How else?

WILLIAM: I don't know, sire. Just else.

RICHARD: No. 'Tis very snug.

WILLIAM: Should we leave you then, O Brightest Stars in the Firmament?

RICHARD: As you wish.

ALICE: We will stay Lord, if you require it.

RICHARD: Excellent.

WILLIAM: Then we'll stay. Shall we stay quiet or what?

RICHARD: Aye, quiet is best. (*Mumbles from inside the canopy.*) Oh no, best make a noise, else we shall not know if you remain.

WILLIAM: What kind of noise, majesty?

RICHARD: Well, something pleasing, mayor. Can you sing?

WILLIAM: No. Not uh singing as such. No.

ALICE (*hissing*): I told you he liked music.

RICHARD: Shame. Just hum then, eh?

WILLIAM: Hum?

RICHARD (*out from the giggles*): Aye, that's it, mayor. You hum for us while your wife gets the supper out for the rabble.

WILLIAM: Oh. (*Doubtfully.*) Right-o, then.

WILLIAM *hums.*

Scene Five

A room in the house of GEOFFREY *and* KATHRYN LE KOLVE.
GEOFFREY LE KOLVE *paces about, agitated. Sitting are* KATHRYN *and* FATHER HENRY MELTON. *They're eating an elaborate meal.*

GEOFFREY: I'll tell you what's happening.

KATHRYN: Oh?

GEOFFREY: He's petitioning the King. That's what. That is what is happening at the Selby house this minute.

KATHRYN: To what end?

GEOFFREY: For my land down Hen Street. Two houses. He's had me in court twice over it and been thrown out. Now he'll petition the King.

KATHRYN: Oh, them! What do you say? Two houses? Two huts you mean, barely stood up. Where you put Thomas and Sarah.

GEOFFREY: Two labourers' houses.

KATHRYN: You don't want them huts, husband. And Thomas could go to your house in Bootham. That's bigger. And empty.

GEOFFREY: I do want 'em! An' I should be Mayor, too. It's my turn. He been Mayor three years. I should be Mayor! Then the King would sleep at our house and I could petition him about my quarrel over the five acres in Stamford Bridge. An' I promised the Bootham house to Walter. So I do want 'em!

KATHRYN: Ease up, husband. You'll be sick.

GEOFFREY: I am sick. (*To* FATHER MELTON.) I prayed over them acres, Pastor; a lot of good it done me.

FATHER MELTON: Pray? how?

GEOFFREY: How? Rosary. Um . . . Novenas. I don't know – plain prayers . . . 'Dear God, let me have that land' prayers. Amen.

FATHER MELTON: For prayers re: land you need a relic of some sort. Let me think . . . Uh! A piece of St Peter's keys. They'll unlock property.

GEOFFREY: Aye?

FATHER MELTON: I have a piece, but 'tis not cheap.

GEOFFREY: To buy?

FATHER MELTON: To kiss. I'll not sell relics. 'Tis corrupt.

GEOFFREY: An' 'tis bad business.

KATHRYN: To think that Alice Selby entertains a King and Queen. It makes me boil.

GEOFFREY: And me.

KATHRYN: Her kitchen's no comparison with mine. Nor her cooks. Nor her hangings. Nor her bed. *And* it's small that house.

GEOFFREY: Oh, 'tain't small.

KATHRYN: 'Tis small. The building is big out but 'tis not big indoors. What do you say, Henry?

FATHER MELTON: Um. I'm not worldly on the size of houses.

KATHRYN: 'Tis good you should have one thing to be not worldly on.

FATHER MELTON: I think so.

KATHRYN: Worse, the woman herself is big outside but small indoors. She buys books and talks a sort of French and understands neither.

GEOFFREY: You set too much store by books, madam. She's a good wife, that mistress. She been more Mayor than him.

KATHRYN: Oh has she? And have *I* not been *your* back legs for twenty year?

GEOFFREY: She's seen at functions.

KATHRYN (*outraged*): And I am seen, sir! And I am seen! I guarantee I am seen at functions *more* even if I attend fewer. Men have washed up at my bosom, Mister. More fellows shipwrecked on me than Alice Selby have anchored with her leaden chat at your precious functioning. Is that not the truth, Father?

FATHER MELTON: Oh. Uh. 'Tis probable.

GEOFFREY: A man cannot succeed in public when his private is wagged from tongue to tongue.

KATHRYN (*in mock outrage*): And what mean you by that, prithee?

GEOFFREY (*backing down*): I should be Mayor, that's all.

KATHRYN: Now you take heed, Mister. I'll not be scape-goat to your thin blood which has more water in it than you cheat into your paint.

GEOFFREY: Enough, woman!

FATHER MELTON: I have counsel could I get a word in edgeways.

KATHRYN: What?

FATHER MELTON: 'Tis simple. Speak to the King yourself. Gain audience. Take gifts. Kathryn will charm him. She has made walls smile; a King should not trouble her. Honeyed so, he will hear your case no less kindly than the Mayor's.

KATHRYN: Better, I should speak to the wife. She has no children. I'll cure that.

FATHER MELTON: No witchery, madam. It's a mortal sin.

KATHRYN: Herbs and good prayer, Father. Not witchery.

GEOFFREY: So you think we should present ourselves? Hmm? At the Mayor's house?

FATHER MELTON: If needs be. Course, if the King stop for the Feast day and sees the plays and like ours . . .

KATHRYN: But where would he watch from? Minster Gates?

FATHER MELTON: Oh no. Above the Common Hall, surely.

GEOFFREY: No. 'Tis uncomfortable there for so long and late in the order. (*Pessimistically.*) No, no doubt he'll stop in Selby's house to watch, and hurrah their pageant and give them my land and champion their Guild and make him Mayor for life and 'Rise, Sir William' and all is utter lost and useless.

KATHRYN: Aye, well that be positive, husband.

GEOFFREY: Well . . .

KATHRYN: First, he could watch the plays elsewhere. Second, he could like your play best. Is it best?

GEOFFREY: Well . . .

KATHRYN: Henry?

FATHER MELTON: 'Tis cheapest.

GEOFFREY: Never!

FATHER MELTON: 'Tis cheap.

KATHRYN (*Machiavellian*): Aye, and this King love a good pageant. 'Tis a sorrow.

GEOFFREY (*bristling*): You could cover our wagon with gold and Will Bluefront and them boys would still look cheap! Great galleybaggers!

FATHER MELTON (*despairing*): Aye. And a fuzz-faced Mary and a fat Christ and the best bits hacked off as saving. Let me have cloth, sir! And gold!

KATHRYN: And change the boys, Geoffrey! If you cannot catch a King on the Cross play . . . aye . . . shoo off the old crew. That's the thing. Walter'll help. Give him the Jesus. He can soft soap the whole business.

GEOFFREY (*sulkily*): I don't know.

KATHRYN: Would scare the back legs off the Mayor and his shrew . . .

FATHER MELTON: That's true.

GEOFFREY (*thawing*): I can't afford to be throwing my money away. Each shilling I make has my sweat on it.

KATHRYN: Aye but 'tis not what you have, chicken, but what you can be *seen* to have. Put your money on the planks and it will be seen!

GEOFFREY: And what if they don't stop? And go home? Then what?

KATHRYN: They'll stop. They must. Do it, husband, and let them hurrah your pageant and give you the Mayor and give you the land and 'Rise, *Sir* Geoffrey!' And all is not lost and utter useless.

FATHER MELTON: Bravo.

KATHRYN (*going to the shuttered window*): We has a stopping place outside. They can watch from upstairs. A King at our window we could charge, we could get . . . what, another twenty pound from our station. Aye: we'll win his favour and flatter his love of the play with our wagon and (*She looks out suddenly and is startled.*) Husband, am I lunatic or is weird scenes going on at the Selby house?

FATHER MELTON: What's afoot?

KATHRYN: Come, both of you! Is that not the Mayor's house and is that not a feast being fed to paupers?

FATHER MELTON (*sorrowfully*): My God, look at them meats.

GEOFFREY: By Christ, there's ten shilling on them plates. Look at them trays. Mutton.

FATHER MELTON: Sturgeon. Venison. Is that venison? I love a hung venison.

GEOFFREY: The blessed Virgin Mary, Mother of God. It's a madness.

FATHER MELTON: What a terrible waste. (*Miserably.*) Quails.

KATHRYN (*a sudden epiphany*): Husband! Quick! Quick!

GEOFFREY: What?

KATHRYN: Call the servants. We must get busy.

GEOFFREY: What's this?

KATHRYN (*pacing*): We've got beef hung for the feast day and two lamb. It's a tragedy but I suppose the cidered ham must go and all.

GEOFFREY: What's this? Go where?

KATHRYN: Call John, quick! And Susan and Sarah, and get them doling out before we lose everything . . .

GEOFFREY: Woman, are you queer?

FATHER MELTON: What ails you, Kathryn?

KATHRYN: Oh, shit. I'll do it myself. I fight a lone war without a man near me with a bean to rattle in his skull. (*Wearily, as if addressing two children.*) If the Mayor dole out food can only be because the King wills it. Therefore we must dole out food an' all, else we lag behind. Do you see? Now get to. (*Calling.*) Sarah! Sarah!

KATHRYN *runs off.*

Scene Six

The Streets.
   ALICE SELBY *and her waiting woman; the* QUEEN *and hers; the two servants behind at some distance.*
   ALICE *is exhausted from this unfamiliar walking.*

ALICE: If Your Majesty tires we could have the horses brought up.

ANNE: Madam, I get sore rump from riding and a joggled view of a place. I like walking.

ALICE (*mournfully*): Oh yes, I love a walk. An' you thirst not, Highness?

ANNE: I thirst for people, mistress. Do you have none in the town?

ALICE: People? Oh aye, we do, many. My husband thought you'd wish the streets clear.

ANNE: Why?

ALICE: We have the usual harvest of lepers and paupers. They affect the view. Also six sergeant run ahead, ma'am, sweeping the walk and shooing beggars. Did the Minster please you, my Lady? 'Tis said if our spire soared taller 'twould tear heaven.

ANNE: I would like it more, mistress, if you would accompany me unaccompanied by your smell. What is it?

ALICE: 'Tis an orange stuck with cloves and rosemary, Majesty, it keeps off infection.

ANNE: No doubt, but it infects me and makes my head ache.

ALICE (*throwing it high behind her*): 'Tis gone, Your Majesty. I beg pardon.

ANNE: No madam, beg not or you will be shooed off by your sergeants. I would like people, if only to measure your spires by.

ALICE: Cicely! Run ahead and tell the men to call out folk to stand against their houses. *Do* you wish any by the Minster, madam? We could return and look again with persons by it.

ANNE: Oh no, let's walk on, eh?

ALICE: 'Tis a very clean town, my Lady. Have you noticed? No pig muck. Nowt. We'll not have it. We have laws for hygiene. My husband made them.

ANNE: What think you when the people make their own laws?

ALICE (*not certain what she's supposed to think*): Um . . . how think you, Your Majesty?

ANNE: I have no quarrel with clean streets.

ALICE: Yes, my husband has achieved much as Mayor. He is out all the hours of the day and if he's not devoting his energies to the town's benefit, then he's in the court up to his girdle in litigation.

ANNE: Oh dear.

ALICE (*transparent*): By coincident we stand by two houses here which belong rightly to my husband and are contested.

ANNE: Which houses?

ALICE: Well . . . more huts, in truth . . . these madam. But for the charge of our lawyer they should be palaces. The business grieves my husband sorely.

ANNE: I'm sorry to hear it.

ALICE: Are you? Are you, Most Beneficint Majesty?

ANNE: Well yes . . . quite sorry.

ALICE: Aye. Them are the two huts of Hen Street. I expect you, like me, hold your man upright?

ANNE: I expect I do, from time to time.

ALICE (*warming to her task*): And I wager . . . just like me . . . you play Virgin to his Christ.

ANNE: How's that, mistress?

ALICE: You know, my Lady: to speak to him they must first speak to me.

ANNE: I see.

ALICE: How long may you stop with us, dear Queen?

ANNE: Oh, I know not. Past the plays, then I know not.

ALICE: Aye, but definite past the pageants then?

ANNE: Aye.

ALICE: Aye. Well, my husband's guild is most proud of its plays. 'Tis most lavish. His plans are most lavish.

ANNE: Your husband, madam, is wonderfully represented by you.

ALICE: Oh. 'Tis strange. Last night I dreamed he were Sir William. I woke with cheeks wet from tears of joy.

ANNE: If he is one quarter of the man you describe, he should be Sir at least.

ALICE (*excited*): Yes! Yes, my Queen! Were he one quarter the man! What keeps Cicely? Let me run ahead and find some folks for you to look at. Will you excuse me, dear lady?

ANNE: I will.

ALICE: *Au revoir, madame.*

ANNE: Yes.

> ALICE *runs off, leaving* ANNE *alone.*
> SARAH ZACHARY *appears.*

> Hello.

SARAH: Your Majesty, I was called out to be looked at.

ANNE: Ah, thank you, and what's your name, mistress?

SARAH: Sarah, madam. Married to Thomas Zachary, labourer.

ANNE: Well, Sarah, would you mind if I leant on you, rather than looked at you?

SARAH: No madam.

ANNE: So Sarah, married to Thomas Zachary, labourer, are you the Mayoress' woman?

SARAH: Oh no, madam, I am in the service of the Master of the Painters' Guild.

ANNE: And is this your house then, there's a fuss over it? (*It is.*)

SARAH: Don't know, madam.

ANNE: I think it is.

SARAH: I think there may be some rivalry between the Masters in the town.

ANNE: I think there may be too, Sarah. Gently put. Now, do you know the route back to the Mayor's house?

SARAH: I do madam, I brought you a letter there this morning from my mistress.

ANNE: A letter?

SARAH: Aye. Inviting you to view the procession of the plays from my master's window.

ANNE: Mmm. Lead me back then Sarah.

> *As they exit.*

SARAH: Certainly, yes madam.

ANNE: And tell me about your mistress, what's she like?

SARAH: Lovely.

ANNE: Lovely? And what else?

SARAH: She has some lovely gowns.

> ANNE *and* SARAH *exit.*

Scene Seven

The Mayor's gardens. A prized lawn.
> RICHARD, OXFORD *and* WILLIAM *appear armed with golf clubs and balls.*

WILLIAM (*cheerfully*): So, my Lord, what is it we aims at? (*Indicating merrily with his club offstage and up.*) The Minster glass! Ha!

OXFORD: He swing that club elegantly, eh sire?

RICHARD: 'Tis a sportsman.

WILLIAM: Well, more a Carlisle axe I'm used to.

OXFORD: Ah, a warrior!

WILLIAM: An' I like a kick at football.

OXFORD: 'Tis banished from London, football.

WILLIAM: Aye, an' here.

OXFORD: The traders say it disturb their stalls.

WILLIAM (*uncomfortably*): Aye.

OXFORD (*pointedly*): They do the same with men who disturb them.

WILLIAM: Aye?

OXFORD (*violently*): Aye, they do. They kick 'em out. Anything which disturbs their pile of coins: out!

WILLIAM: So, this golf, my Lords: a case of he who sends the ball furthest, is it?

RICHARD: Oh no, 'tis not a show of strength, Mayor, but of elegance. 'Tis one sport where brute force is not everything. No, 'tis a hole we need for a beginning.

WILLIAM: A hole? What kind of hole, Majesty?

RICHARD: Oh, a small one. Here will do nicely.

WILLIAM: This is my green, sire. 'Tis prized.

RICHARD: Aye, 'tis perfect for the game, Mayor. Congratulations. Have you seen a better green, Robert?

OXFORD: Never.

RICHARD: Nor me. Shall we start then, or must I admire your grass further?

WILLIAM (*tragically*): No. I'll just dig up a hole then. Here, you say?

RICHARD: Don't set to yourself, Mayor. You're playing. Have a boy out with a trowel. Otherwise every time we need another hole you'll be too occupied gardening to play.

WILLIAM: How many of these holes do we need?

RICHARD: As we like, Mayor. As we like.

WILLIAM: I'll get a boy, then. And a trowel. Excuse me, my lords.

WILLIAM *exits, leaving* RICHARD *and* OXFORD *alone.*

OXFORD: 'Tis almost sad were it not for his vileness.

The Queen enters.

ANNE: My lords, no golf?

RICHARD: We're due, madam. We wait on the holes.

ANNE: Ah. And how do the holes go down with the Mayor?

RICHARD: Deep, madam, deep.

OXFORD: His heart thump so, we fear it may thump out.

ANNE: No matter. His wife approaches and will have him canonized directly.

WILLIAM *returns with a servant.*

RICHARD: Ah, Mayor.

WILLIAM: Dig here, boy.

RICHARD: Aye lad: a hole the size of your fist and the length of your arm to the elbow.

The boy sets to work.

ANNE: Good day, Mayor.

WILLIAM: Oh, Majesty, forgive me! My mind wanders.

ANNE: Aye, well, how could you notice me? I am not at grass level.

WILLIAM: No. (*Wincing at the hole.*) Enough! (*Then anxiously to the King:*) Surely?

RICHARD: A finger more, I reckon. Eh, Robert?

OXFORD: Aye, a thumb.

RICHARD: That's it. Now, Mayor. Over here and tap your ball to the hole. He who sinks his ball with least strokes, wins. You begin.

WILLIAM: Oh no. You must start, sire.

RICHARD: No. You.

WILLIAM: I couldn't.

RICHARD: Start!

WILLIAM: As Your Majesty bids. (*He makes a good putt.*)

ANNE: Well done, Mayor!

RICHARD: Aye, well hit! Now me. (*He makes a bad putt.*)

WILLIAM: Good, Majesty.

RICHARD: No, sir. Bad.

WILLIAM: Aye, well: quite good.

RICHARD: Robert . . .

ROBERT *makes a good putt.*

RICHARD: Bravo. 'Tis your hit, Mister.

WILLIAM: Aye.

OXFORD: And you should win with it.

WILLIAM *misses, quite deliberately, when it would be easier to sink his putt.*

WILLIAM: No.

OXFORD: The idea of the game, Mister, is to get your ball down the hole.

WILLIAM: Aye. 'Tis Your Majesty next.

RICHARD *casually and deliberately misses.*

RICHARD: Missed, dammit. 'Tis your victory Oxford.

OXFORD: Aye, I'd say so.

OXFORD *plays the ball behind his back and misses.*

OXFORD: Oh gross *merde* of a Turkish donkey! Ah well, a formality, Mayor.

WILLIAM: Is it my hit again? Surely 'tis yours, Majesty!

RICHARD: No.

WILLIAM: I think I just had mine, sire.

ANNE: You did and then the King did and then Robert did. 'Tis you again.

WILLIAM *mournfully taps the ball into the hole.*

RICHARD: You won, Mayor.

WILLIAM: I'm sorry, Your Majesty.

RICHARD: Hm. This hole poxes me. Let's make another.

WILLIAM: Another, Majesty?

RICHARD: Aye. A new one.

WILLIAM: Boy, dig another hole.

The servant trowels out another hole.

ANNE: How do you like golf, Mayor?

WILLIAM: Merrily.

RICHARD: You like it merrily? Good. What should I bestow on you now you've won a hole?

WILLIAM: Nothing, Majesty, other than your favour.

ANNE: Should you be hurt, husband, that the Mayor counts your favour so close to nothing?

OXFORD: More hurt he refuses a gift from you when he has a-showered you with trinkets.

RICHARD: Aye. I think I sulk somewhat.

WILLIAM: Please sire. Forgive me. I'd delight in a gift.

RICHARD: What would you like then, Mister?

WILLIAM: Um . . .

RICHARD: Name anything.

WILLIAM: I had a case at law, sir. I squabble over houses down Hen Street. I want 'em, my lord, and so do some other bugger.

There is a pause.

RICHARD: 'Tis greedy, sir.

WILLIAM: Is it?

RICHARD: What think you, madam?

ANNE: 'Tis a little greedy.

WILLIAM: Aye, you're right sire. 'Tis gross.

OXFORD: True, Mayor . . . not a little greedy: *gross* greedy.

WILLIAM: I'm sorry. I'll drop the suit.

RICHARD: Then let that be my gift: to encourage your generosity.

WILLIAM: Thank you, sire. Thank you. I love this golf. The whole town will be at golf soon. No pageants soon, for golf games.

RICHARD: Keep the pageant, sir.

WILLIAM (*quickly*): Right.

RICHARD: I like a play more than anything.

WILLIAM: And I do. And I do. Oh aye. Love a play.

RICHARD: Last year I were at Coventry.

WILLIAM: I heard, sire.

ANNE: The play there is excellent.

WILLIAM: And here, sire. Excellent.

RICHARD: What does your Guild present? (*He goes to the new hole.*) I like not this hole. Let's have another.

WILLIAM (*gloomily*): Another.

RICHARD: Aye.

WILLIAM: We could return to the first, sire, and begin again a new round.

RICHARD: No. A new one, eh Robert?

OXFORD: Oh yes. Definite.

RICHARD: You didn't speak of your pageant, sir.

WILLIAM (*gloomily*): Oh, 'tis the '*Slaughter of the Innocent*', sir.

RICHARD: Ah, the Herod play. Wondrous Herod at Coventry. Very fine. Hair as red as a furnace.

WILLIAM: Oh, wait till you see ours, sire. 'Tis furious red.

RICHARD: Good. You to start, Mayor.

WILLIAM: Right.

They're putting only from a few yards. WILLIAM *holes in one.*

ANNE: Oh Mayor! Well hit!

WILLIAM: Oh. A fluke, Majesty. Not intended.

RICHARD: 'Tis the object, Mayor. What did you intend?

WILLIAM: Oh aye, 'tis the object, I know. I intended to be very close with my first hit. Oh.

At this ALICE *appears.*

ALICE: Majesties. My Lord. Husband. How is the golf?

ANNE: Your husband plays the game as well as he mayors, madam.

ALICE: Do he! (*Delighted, to* WILLIAM.) And have you given the King his winnings?

WILLIAM: Uh.

RICHARD: I win not, madam. In fact, I lose.

ALICE: Husband, is this true? Do you let a King lose?

WILLIAM: Uh.

OXFORD: He beats us both, madam. Skilfully.

WILLIAM: As gift for my winnings, sire, could I retreat now and count my blessings?

RICHARD: Aye, retreat.

ALICE (*furiously*): NO, Mister. You must play again. Do you need a new hole, Majesty?

RICHARD: Aye.

ALICE: Dig some more holes, Adam. Several.

ANNE: Your husband was just saying how much he liked the game.

ALICE: I bet. I mean, 'tis a Royal sport.

ANNE: Aye.

ALICE: Aye. I'd like to play myself, me. Do women, madam?

ANNE: Oh, I expect so.

ALICE: Then I'll learn.

ANNE: Splendid. In fact, mistress, as your husband has such a talent let him show you. My husband and the Earl will come with me now and I'll pass on the joys of our walk. (*She beams at* RICHARD.) Husband, give the lady your club.

OXFORD: An' here's mine!

ALICE: But Majesties!

ANNE: No buts! 'Tis our pleasure, eh my lords?

RICHARD: Aye. We insist.

WILLIAM: Uh.

RICHARD: What's that, Mayor?

WILLIAM: Nothing, Majesty.

ANNE: So . . . adieu, mistress. Mayor.

OXFORD: Aye. Have fun.

    RICHARD, OXFORD *and* ANNE *exit, gaily.*

ALICE (*furiously*): Ach, William can I ask you a simple question? How is it you have not even the guile to manage to lose a game you cannot play!

WILLIAM (*heavily*): Boy: stop digging up my green, please, and go away.

    The servant exits.

ALICE (*with club and ball*): *Alors.* I just aims at the hole, do I?

WILLIAM: Madam, my patience is gouged. 'Tis a veritable sieve.

ALICE (*concentrating*): Aye? (*She hits the ball well.*) Heigh-ho.

WILLIAM (*very ill*): How many year do I breed this grass, madam?

ALICE (*sinking her putt*): There!

WILLIAM (*exploding*): OH GOD!!

    WILLIAM *whacks a ball offstage. There is a glorious smashing of glass.*

    (*Funereally.*) Oh, no.

ALICE (*looking, and nodding gravely*): 'Tis the Minster glass, William. 'Tis holed in one.

ACT TWO

Scene One

The week of the play.
   WALTER's *workshop. Early morning.*
   Behind a screen WALTER *tries on the Mary costume while* SARAH *waits.*

SARAH: How is it, Master Walter?

WALTER: It don't fit, Sarah. I am grown at the shoulder since last year.

SARAH: Aye.

WALTER: And at the stomach. I can scarce breathe in it. (*He comes out, awkward, coy.*) I feel a right clot.

SARAH: You'll live.

WALTER: I pass for Mary?

SARAH: I think so. (*Adjusting her dress.*) Mistress Eleanor has made a man of you.

WALTER (*lightly*): Then I love her for others will only make a woman of me.

SARAH (*hurt*): That is not fair, Walter!

WALTER: I tease you.

SARAH: Well, you should not. 'Tis a raw thing.

WALTER (*taken aback*): Are you not happy wife to your Tom?

SARAH: I am.

WALTER: Well then.

SARAH: All the same, you should not tease.

WALTER: Oh Sarah. 'Tis long gone all that. Surely?

SARAH: Oh. Surely. (*Pause. Adjusting the dress. Simply.*) You look beautiful.

WALTER: What? With my beard?

SARAH: Aye, with your wee beard and your blue veil. I know you could not wed me, Walter. 'Tis one world to serve and another to be served. 'Tis not your fault.

WALTER (*awkward*): Well . . .

SARAH: I said to Mistress Eleanor I'd stitch her clothes for the church door.

WALTER: She said. 'Tis generous.

SARAH: And I'll make the christening gown, too.

WALTER: Madam you need not sew us into the sheets.

SARAH: No.

GEOFFREY (*off*): Walter?

WALTER: In here, master.

GEOFFREY (*off, nearer*): Walter?

WALTER: Here, sir.

   GEOFFREY *and* FATHER MELTON *enter together.*

GEOFFREY: Ah Walter. (*To* SARAH:) 'Morning, Sarah. (*Then inquiringly, to* WALTER:) Do the merchants come for the Herod face?

WALTER: Aye. 'Tis wondrous red locks they bring for it: fresh cropped.

SARAH: Aye. 'Tis Edward's wife's hair. She sold it to pay for their bairn.

WALTER: No!

SARAH: Aye.

FATHER MELTON: See, mister, they lavish on their pageant.

SARAH: They do, mister. We heard they have new hose for the Jews and send for armour from Beverley.

GEOFFREY: Ach!

FATHER MELTON (*of* WALTER): See, Geoffrey. The boy grows too much boy for the Blessed Virgin.

SARAH: I do redress the dress, Father.

FATHER MELTON (*doubtfully*): But the face, too . . .

GEOFFREY: Walter, the merchants will outplay us; they plan to bring in their Herod, and the Kings, and will have a maid to play the Mother.

WALTER: Never!

FATHER MELTON: In London, Walter, the wives play the Assumption themselves. They know the King's likings and pander. So must we.

WALTER: So I am dumped, then?

GEOFFREY: Not dumped. We'll make a Jesus of you.

FATHER MELTON: 'Tis what you will.

SARAH: And Thomas?

GEOFFREY: We propose you to play the Mary, Sarah. You has a clear voice and fair face, and we hear the Queen smiled on you . . .

WALTER: And Thomas?

FATHER MELTON: Our scheme is to change all the men. Not just Thomas.

WALTER: How change?

FATHER MELTON: We search for new soldiers and may use the players from De La Poles of Hull.

WALTER: Minstrels?

GEOFFREY: No, proper players and highly spoke of. Will cost us eight pound.

WALTER: And why spend eight pound, pray, when your current men know the pageant and love it and are the pride of the Pinners and Painters?

FATHER MELTON: *Parce-que*, Walter, 'tis a play before a King.

WALTER: Does he not value these qualities?

SARAH: I think he do.

GEOFFREY: Think, Mister, of the merchants' might. If we stick to our humble fair 'tis comparison of donkey with stallion.

WALTER: 'Tis a town, Mister, of citizens not knights, and thus have more use of donkeys. In my view.

FATHER MELTON: You wished to speak for Christ, Walter. Now you can. Your Thomas has played him too long, Sarah. 'Tis a young man's part. We all know it. And the cuts are restored. And the cloth. I have this new notion for the Christ's cloak. 'Tis so: Walter come on wrapped in the small purple. After he lay on the tree and the soldiers come to dice for it, 'tis picked up and on a sudden is lengths and lengths long.

SARAH: How?

FATHER MELTON: I have a method for substitution. The crowd will watch the *crucifying*, not the cloth.

WALTER: The business of the cloth, Parson, is similar to the business of the play. A week ago were subject to cuts, now is to be enlarged beyond belief.

FATHER MELTON: This Christ you will play, Walter, will be all gold on the planks; not simply the mask. And despite the buffeting will not be racked but will rest transcendent on the tree while the purple cloth billows out beneath him.

GEOFFREY: So . . .

WALTER: And our rehearsal?

GEOFFREY: Oh, rehearse! No harm done in that. Besides, Da La Poles may not appear. No, rehearse. Don't want to upset the cart just yet, Walter.

WALTER: Then excuse me, Mister, pardon.

GEOFFREY: Aye.

FATHER MELTON: I'll follow shortly.

SARAH: May I go now an' all, sir?

GEOFFREY: Aye, do. But be bound to say nothing to the others, now.

SARAH: Aye, sir.

> WALTER *and* SARAH *exit.*
> GEOFFREY *and* FATHER MELTON *ruminate.*

FATHER MELTON: Hm.

GEOFFREY: The girl can be replaced. 'Tis a sop, in case the Queen do like her. Walter'll do it.

FATHER MELTON: I'm not so certain.

GEOFFREY: Oh I am, me. He'll want to get on. Aye, well if he don't, there's plenty who will. Forget this rehearsal, Chaplain, and get word to Hull. And see if you can't get them for seven pound, eh?

> GEOFFREY *and* FATHER MELTON *exit.*

Scene Two

The Streets.
> SARAH *and a befrocked* WALTER *are on their way to rehearsal.*

SARAH: An' will you?

WALTER: Will I what?

SARAH: Play the Christ instead of my Thomas?

WALTER: I play the fool parading the streets in this frock. I may do. I may die. I don't know. Will you play the Virgin?

SARAH: Walter, I think gold Christs and flows of purple is plays for Italians and not for farthing folk who pack the station at Corpus Christi.

WALTER: Aye. I know, Sarah. Edward, who is a saint in my mind – Edward speak of playing the plays with such joy. He hath but few words in it and they gross and cruel but his cheeks ruddy as the pageant draw out next Thursday. 'Tis our man from our guild, as they all be, and all should be.

SARAH: Then you'll say no.

They walk towards the Pageant House.

WALTER (*uncertainly*): Aye . . . well, I may do.

The rehearsal takes place outside the Pageant House. The wagon is dragged out ready. The players, WILL, EDWARD, THOMAS, sit happily on the wagon, as WALTER and SARAH approach.

THOMAS: Wife, who is this beauty you've brought?

WILL: Has a fine rump on her . . . How do, ladies?

WALTER: How do, Edward?

EDWARD (*laughing at him a little*): Well, Walter. An' you?

WALTER: Weary.

WILL: We'll have no sulking this morning, nips. Edward's missus sends us great cake. Thomas is happy. I knows my part backward and the day blesses us.

WALTER: Then let's start.

SARAH: May I watch, gentlemen?

WILL: Aye. Be our audience. (*To* WALTER:) And don't tell us you have more changes. Keep that parson out and let's get on with the pageant.

WALTER: Let's begin then.

THOMAS: Aye.

WILL (*imitating the trumpet fanfare, then announcing proudly*): The Play of the Pinners, Latterners and Painters: Christ Crucified.

What follows is a version of the York play No. 35, Crux, Jesus Extensus in ea super terram . . . *In the rehearsal the play is performed humbly, earnestly and as beautifully as possible from beginning to end. The performance of* WILL, EDWARD *and company is broad, familiar and skilful. The original play is extraordinary. My version is faithful to its content and style and idiom.*

The Passion Play

The two soldiers enter followed by a bloodied Christ, (THOMAS), *heaving the cross.*

SOLDIER ONE (*played by* WILL): This way then nipper. Up on this hill lay down
the tree
and strip to stripéd skin.

SOLDIER TWO (*played by* EDWARD): I've brought stubs to nail him up and mallet
to mash them in.

SOLDIER ONE: I've brought rope to bind him
and crown to crown him
and himself cross to cross him.

SOLDIER TWO: By Christ, he do blaspheme and calls hisself
many things
as Saviour, King and God's son.

SOLDIER ONE: What say you sir to this event?
Are you King? And will you rule from this
tree your kingdom?

SOLDIER TWO: He calls himself nowt now but plays the fool.
Let's have him up and hear him sing.
I'll bang the holes in with this tool
and stretch him out and pull and pull.
(*He bangs at the cross to make the bore holes*)

SOLDIER ONE: Aye, you do that while I crown his head
and thorn him bloody, thorn him red.

> Till red runs down him, joins the stream
> into a river bed.
> Hail King, Hail Fool, Hail Witch, Hail Pleb!
> (*He crowns Christ, with the crown
> of thorns*)

SOLDIER TWO (*to Christ*): Come bend your back to this tree.

Christ obeys.

SOLDIER ONE: An' he do, an' he do, quiet as a lamb, see!

SOLDIER TWO: I'll do his hands.

SOLDIER ONE: I'll do his feet.

SOLDIER TWO: Cross them and save one nail.

SOLDIER ONE: What? Bash it through the two?

SOLDIER TWO: Aye, bash it through the two.

SOLDIER ONE: Then that's what I'll do, though 'tis a to-do.

SOLDIER TWO (*having difficulty as he nails Christ to the cross.*)
Oh shit, that's a pain
I've not judged the holes right

SOLDIER ONE: Then stretch him again
and yank him to that side.

SOLDIER TWO: Done it! by Christ! and broken the bone.

SOLDIER ONE: To lug him down here
I've broken the toes
and smashed all the sinew.

SOLDIER TWO: I'm knackered.

SOLDIER ONE: I'm puffed.

SOLDIER TWO: We'll never lift him.

SOLDIER ONE: And he can't lift hisself now.
That's a sin.

SOLDIER TWO: Well let's go for company to help do this deed.

SOLDIER ONE: Aye, that's what we need
to mount King onto steed.

SOLDIER TWO: Aye, let's not strain our souls
for the sake of this dolt.
By Christ, he's a do
for four, let alone two.

SOLDIER ONE *exits, then returns, bringing on two other soldiers, non-speaking*

SOLDIER ONE: Come on you boys
and help heave him high
he's off to the tournament
between land and sky.

SOLDIER TWO (*investigating*): Have they had his tongue out?
He were such a loud mouth.

SOLDIER ONE: We'll soon make him sound
when we throw him hard down.

SOLDIER TWO: Up boys up.

SOLDIER ONE: Heave boys heave!

SOLDIER TWO: By Christ, he's a bugger!

SOLDIER ONE: Let's drop him again.

SOLDIER TWO: See how he do shudder.

SOLDIER ONE: That hurt him! That pained!

SOLDIER TWO: Blast! I've done my shoulder.

SOLDIER ONE: Shit! I've done my back.

SOLDIER TWO (*kicking the cross*): You sod!

SOLDIER ONE: You turd.

SOLDIER TWO: You've got a nerve.

SOLDIER ONE: Call yourself God!

SOLDIER TWO: Ha! Now he do whimper
                  Were he a real God he'd simper!

SOLDIER ONE: Ha! How he do moan.
                  So much for your throne.

SOLDIER TWO: Where is his soldiers come to rescue him?

SOLDIER ONE (*spearing Christ's side*): Here's his banner though:
                  This red flag on his bones.

SOLDIER TWO (*as they exit*): Come along, boys, let's leave this scene
                  We'll raffle his cloak for a flagon.
                  He's not going to sing, is he
                  Or jump down from our wagon.
                  This so-called King is a worm, not a dragon.
                  And we've threaded him here on the tree
                  So all he'll catch is the sun
                  All he'll catch is his breath
                  All he'll catch is his death and that slowly.

    The two soldiers exit.
      CHRIST *is left alone on the cross, but as he speaks* MARY (WALTER) *enters*

CHRIST: Ah . . .
                  Father
                  Forgive them their cruelty.
                  They know nothing of me.
                  They here have me tree'd.
                  For Adam's sin I now bleed
                  and tremble and bleed
                  and pray you will speed
                  to release me from this pain.
                  Your son swoons dear Lord
                  and I pray
                  that all that I suffer may not be in vain
                  but bring down your mercy on men
                  like an endless cleansing rain.

MARY: Alas, my love, my love, my Liege.
                  Alas, mourning now maddens me.
                  Alas, my boy look down on me,
                  Thy mother that did bear thee.
                  You are my fruit, I fostered thee,
                  and gave thee suck upon my knee.
                  Upon my pain have pity.
                  Alas to find my boy –

WALTER *is interrupted in mid-pieta by a suffering* THOMAS.

THOMAS: Ow! Walter I must get down!

WALTER: What?

WILL (*angry*): What's he yoppeling?

SARAH (*worried*): Tom?

THOMAS (*urgently. During this*): I must come down. I've got cramps all up my leg.

WALTER: Oh right.

WILL: You can't! He can't!

THOMAS: I has to, Will. Ow! Help me!

WILL: You can't get off the cross in the middle of the pageant!

THOMAS: I 'ave to, Will. I'm buggered. Yow!

EDWARD: Ease up, Will. 'Tis only a rehearsal. Come on, Tom, I've got you.

They begin to get TOM *down.*

WILL: Ach! It were going perfect. Come on then, Galleybag.

They lower the cross.

SARAH: You all right, lovely?

THOMAS: Ow! Ow! Ow! Don't touch my leg!

The others laugh.

EDWARD: Tom, you're dancing! In't he, eh!

THOMAS: Don't touch my leg!

Much merriment as THOMAS *dances.*

Scene Three

The Le Kolves' bedroom. Early morning.
     KATHRYN LE KOLVE *and* FATHER MELTON *are in bed. They both wear shifts and take it in turn to delouse each other.*

KATHRYN: I must get myself to the Queen.

FATHER MELTON: And I to the chapel.

KATHRYN: The bugs seem to love this cloth particular. (*Meaning his shift.*)

FATHER MELTON: Is my hair busy?

KATHRYN (*exploring and finding a bug*): Here's a plump boy! (*She pops it.*) Aye. I will say I like the look of the Earl. He has a fine leg on him.

FATHER MELTON (*producing his leg*): Do I?

KATHRYN: Very fine but not so influential.

FATHER MELTON: Madam, I have access to God . . . 'tis more influence than with any King.

KATHRYN: Aye, but less rare.

FATHER MELTON: How less rare?

KATHRYN: Half the town has the Holy Orders. Only Robert has the King's.

FATHER MELTON: True.

GEOFFREY (*off*): Madam.

KATHRYN: Sir.

GEOFFREY (*off*): Are you a-bed still?

KATHRYN: Aye.

GEOFFREY (*off*): Is the priest with you?

KATHRYN: Aye, he ministers to me.

GEOFFREY (*off*): Does he?

KATHRYN: Both to my soul, sir, and to my bugs.

GEOFFREY (*off*): Can I come up?

KATHRYN (*laughing*): No. (*To* FATHER MELTON:) Not when my soul is bared so.

GEOFFREY (*off*): What's that?

KATHRYN: We shall be down by and by, sirrah. (*To* FATHER MELTON:) Cover yourself up, Henry.

GEOFFREY (*off*): We are appointed to attend the Royal Party in the hour.

KATHRYN (*as they dress*): If you are happy to bellow, Mister, we need not dress ourselves but simply stay here and converse with their Majesties so.

GEOFFREY (*off*): What, pray, madam, is a husband to do when his wife forbids him entry to the bedroom and then lives her life there?

KATHRYN: If I could learn you one thing, Mister, it is that nothing was ever solved by whining. 'Tis a dog's solution and not a man's.

GEOFFREY (*off*): Ach!

KATHRYN (*to* FATHER MELTON): I think he quiets. (*She listens.*) Yes. 'Tis the whining I can't forgive him for. That and the excessive sweat he make. Unnerve him, Parson, and the liquid dribbles from him. Or excite him, the same. 'Tis hard to clasp a man to you, so slippery.

FATHER MELTON: What wear you to the King?

KATHRYN: Oh, nothing grand, but look . . . (*She gets up from the bed and fishes around in the chest at its foot.*) How do you like this, Henry? (*It's a large silk handkerchief. She waves it above her head.*)

GEOFFREY *bursts in, clutching a bale of cloth.*

(*Glowering.*) You burst in on us, Mister. I like not to be burst in on.

GEOFFREY: This has just arrived madam. Think of me as fetcher and carrier. (*He indicates the cloth.*)

FATHER MELTON: 'Tis the cloak, Kathryn. Marvellous.

GEOFFREY: Is so much cloth necessary? 'Tis like the Red Sea.

KATHRYN: Except purple.

FATHER MELTON: Are you not stunned by it, sir?

GEOFFREY: I am stunned more by its cost.

FATHER MELTON: Will not be torn, sir. Can be re-used each year. In time 'twill be cheap. Look at it, Kathryn: Beautiful: Beautiful.

GEOFFREY: I'm just saying it won't be cheap in my time.

KATHRYN: Mister, you will bless us for the cost when the King stand by you and gasp at the spectacle.

GEOFFREY: If he comes.

KATHRYN: He will come. Don't doubt it, sir.

GEOFFREY: Aye well, I liked things as they were, when Kings were Kings and a play had less effect and more language.

KATHRYN: Yes, sir, you has the taste of a labourer!

GEOFFREY: Aye, I has!

KATHRYN: Be educated, sir!

GEOFFREY: Madam, I fork out for your niceties, there is not fat for mine.

KATHRYN: Geoffrey, you are so *pickled*!

GEOFFREY: 'An you would be! My fellows blame me for the cost, my workers set a-mumbling if I enter the shop. My best apprentice will not swap words at all, I am banned from my wife's bedroom when other folk seem welcome and I am faulted for being pickled. I am pickled!

KATHRYN: Husband, we all bear crosses.

GEOFFREY: Aye, well Walter won't bear his. Have you heard that? He won't play the Christ. Makes you wonder, don't it? Makes you bloody wonder!

KATHRYN: I have Sarah sullen, and the taxing friendship of a monarch in prospect. Nor am I best well.

FATHER MELTON: Please, peace, please! The pageant will be true reward for all our efforts. 'Tis certain our play is a star will outshine all others. I have eyes and ears about the Merchants' rehearsals. They have a vulgar Herod who will say too much, too loud. By contrast we will seem an elegance.

GEOFFREY: Well, I'm not elegant, me. It would seem more elegance to me were my wife to drape this purple about herself and not the pageant. But I don't know the fashion. I'll get off and leave you to your fashion. Whatever it is.

GEOFFREY *exits sadly.*

Scene Four

The Mayor's house. The bedroom.
ANNE *delouses* RICHARD *who delouses* OXFORD. *All are sitting on the bed.*

ANNE: Husband, you're crawling.

RICHARD: 'Tis the region, madam. I was clear in London.

ANNE: Oh sir, that's false: no less than your subjects swarm to feed on you do the fleas come nibbling. You are King to too much life.

RICHARD: Well, I like not being either host to the fleas nor guest of the Mayor.

ANNE: Would you rather to the Abbey?

RICHARD: God, no.

OXFORD: Where is the Archbishop?

RICHARD: At war, somewhere. For a man ordained to save souls, he spends much time despatching them to the fires. 'Tis a hard man and a friend now of Gloucester's and Henry Bolingbroke.

OXFORD: And no friend of mine.

RICHARD: No. He would be Bishop of Westminster and Cardinal. He thinks you barred his way when you were at Court.

OXFORD: I did. I would have him Bishop of the Channel and swim in his parish.

ANNE: Robert!

OXFORD: Well I would. 'Tis a lunatic church, madam, and Christ must wonder wide-eyed at us. We have two popes: the Frenchman a butcher, the Italian an oaf. And under their gaze the church is mother to a guild of tinkers and tonsured criminals for whom heaven hath arrived prematurely on earth. To call her corrupt is to call water wet and fire hot. His grace the Archbishop has more land than a Lord *and* more army. He is further from God than the flea.

ANNE (*teasing*): You like him little then?

OXFORD (*laughing*): Aye. Little. He and his like marooned me from you both and would again.

RICHARD: Your head is deserted, Robert. The bugs find little to feast on in your hair, 'tis too acid there.

OXFORD: Aye.

ANNE: Who will search me?

OXFORD: Us both. Ah, here's a lizard!

RICHARD: And here's a toad!

ANNE: Away! You're toads the pair of you and I'll not tolerate your toady hands leaping on me.

RICHARD: Toady, toady. (*He tickles* ANNE.)

OXFORD: Toady, toady. (*He, too tickles* ANNE.)

ANNE: Get off! Anyway, the song of toads is not 'toady, toady'. So there.

RICHARD: I did not know my Queen was an expert on the toad.

ANNE: Sir, I married one (*A beat.*) and he turned into a prince.

OXFORD: Bravo.

RICHARD: Madam, you are a joy.

ANNE: Am I? Then I am a joy with a headache. So let us give audience to these painters and get us back to bed.

RICHARD: Why are we meeting painters?

ANNE: Because it suits me!

RICHARD: Oh?

ANNE: And to keep the waters agitate. A calm surface would show our Mayor the measure of his folly. This painter is his rival. Let's have them all in, let's have their beds.

RICHARD: More beds?

ANNE: The painter's wife begs me to visit hers. I have a letter from her. They would we watch the pageant from their station.

OXFORD: She writes? Perhaps *I* should visit her bed.

ANNE: 'Tis not the pen you would mingle with, Oxford.

OXFORD: One can mingle with a horse, my Lady, 'tis the conversation one misses.

RICHARD: Then let us dress ourselves and be kingly for the painter.

ANNE: I shall go with the mistress, sir. You seduce the man. We'll swap joys later. Will you give me leave?

RICHARD: Aye Madam.

RICHARD *and* ANNE *kiss.*

But dally not with your sore head.

ANNE: Robert.

OXFORD: Adieu, my Lady.

ANNE *exits.*

Sometimes me thinks your Queen is wan, sir, and trembles.

RICHARD: Aye. In the night she grows hot then icy and cries out. The physician bleeds her but does not help, nor quicksilver neither, nor gold. Her health is all my prayer.

OXFORD: And mine too.

RICHARD: I love her laugh more than the world and will clown all day to hear it. So long as she smiles let's sojourn here.

OXFORD: And then?

RICHARD: And then back to London and the penitent burghers. 'Tis the season of stubbornness. 'Twill pass as certain as spring follows winter.

OXFORD: 'Tis not long since you were drowned by this stubbornness.

RICHARD: Was I? Come friend, let's paint this painter a Royal portrait. Is there a crown for me?

OXFORD: There is, sire.

RICHARD: Then crown me and call in a page or two for the proper effect. Were we in London we could run to a few trumpets and bugger the parliament.

OXFORD *obliges.*

Scene Five

Downstairs in the Mayor's house.
    ALICE *enters to find a weary, miserable* WILLIAM.

ALICE: Husband! How is it with you?

WILLIAM: Pricked, madam, sorely.

ALICE: Pricked?

WILLIAM: Aye. Like my grass.

ALICE: Why so gloomy, Mister?

WILLIAM: Ach! Half my trinkets and best relics dropped on His Majesty without effect. My thorn from Christ's crown: Pfft! Gone. And now His Majesty entertains Le Kolve and his missus by and by. 'Tis forgone between them will lard their way into his pleasure.

ALICE: I think no, sir. I think we shall outmethod them. I come via the seamstress. I have collected our wipes. And she tells me they have new costumes for the Painters' pageant and a great cloth. I worry not. We has a great Herod.

WILLIAM (*proudly*): Aye! And we have machines and devices! We have fabulous costumes!

ALICE: That's it, sir! Worry not on our standing. I'll outgrease Mistress Le Kolve. I am already confided of headaches and so forth from upstairs. 'Tis a young woman who wants a friend. I'll be it.

JOLYF ABSOLOM *enters, dressed in the Herod costume, carrying his mask.*

JOLYF: May I punctuate sir? I come for your feeling re: our rehearsal.

WILLIAM: Come in, Come in, Master Absolom. Your Herod is a marvel, most monstrous roar and all.

ALICE: Aye marvellous, and with exploding arse: most devilish!

JOLYF *looks proudly at the fireworks attached to the back of his costume.*

JOLYF: So Your Worships is pleased?

WILLIAM: Oh aye. 'Twere a good rehearsal this morning.

JOLYF: Aye. 'Twas a ripe showing.

WILLIAM: Show us again.

JOLYF *dons his mask.*

Ha! 'Tis a marvel.

JOLYF *roars obligingly and lengthily.*

Aye, enough now.

JOLYF: I am particular pleased with my new phrases.

WILLIAM: Oh?

JOLYF: I bring an extra speech or two with me.

WILLIAM: Oh.

ALICE: Aye, husband, like he refer to York and to our King an' all.

WILLIAM: Oh aye. Aye. Well made.

JOLYF: In truth, though I want not coin for it, I've exchanged a move here and a move there and a manner. 'Tis better for it.

ALICE: Well, Mister, my husband did say this morning of your high fee but evident you earn it.

JOLYF: I do, madam. You'd pay as much elsewhere for the voice alone. With me you get fireworks and new words. 'Tis a complete service.

WILLIAM: Tell me, sir, how compares now our pageant with Coventry?

JOLYF: Well, sir, your Herod is superior. And if he is, the pageant is. I'd say 'tis more fearsome than Coventry.

WILLIAM: Is it?

JOLYF: Should I share a secret or would you be surprised on the day?

WILLIAM: No, say sir. On the day we has ceremony to stand on and would not be surprised.

JOLYF: We plant our women in the crowd at each station.

ALICE: Ha!

JOLYF: Aye, but here's the rub. Each has in her bundle a pig's bladder loaded with gore. So when the soldiers come to slaughter the Innocents, each dip his sword to the bundle like so: in! and splash guts all over the crowd and carry off his bloodied sword aloft.

ALICE: Oh.

JOLYF: Aye, 'tis effective. I anticipate swooning.

ALICE: So do I, sir.

KATHRYN *and* GEOFFREY LE KOLVE *enter.*

KATHRYN (*briskly*): Felicitations, sir, and how do? Dear sister, a gift! (*She thrusts some flowers into* ALICE's *hand.*) Picked from our gardens in Hen Street.

ALICE: *Merci.*

KATHRYN: 'Tis a shame your garden is pock-marked so.

GEOFFREY: How do, Your Worship.

WILLIAM: How do, master. The Queen descends, madam, and will enter shortly. My garden is dug for golf.

KATHRYN: Golf? (*Anxious not to be out-knowledged.*) Oh aye, Golf. (*She pronounces it as if it were French.*) Do we intrude, madam? You seem burdened with show business.

WILLIAM: This is Master Absolom.

GEOFFREY: How do?

WILLIAM: We was just showing him the Herod mask.

ALICE: And you've been keeping the drapers busy, we hear.

KATHRYN: Oh . . . (*Shrugging.*) is your pageant prepared?

WILLIAM: We are so pecked by civic affairs we have small appetite for such luxuries. And yours?

GEOFFREY: Oh, apparently 'tis fine. How goes our play, Kathryn?

KATHRYN: Fair, I think. Humble.

ALICE: Well we was just speaking how much we look forward to viewing it.

KATHRYN: Then 'tis coincidence mistress. We was just relishing yours.

ANNE (*off*): Mistress Selby:

ALICE (*simpering*): I am called. (*Shouting.*) I come, my Queen. *Excusez-moi.*

KATHRYN (*producing a large handkerchief*): *Tout à l'heure.*

ALICE (*producing a larger handkerchief*): *Tout à l'heure.*

KATHRYN *scowls.*

JOLYF: I'll withdraw an' all.

KATHRYN: Don't mind us, we're just passing. We have royal business you see.

JOLYF: No, no, I'll retreat. I'll make an exit.

WILLIAM: Aye, sir, retreat.

JOLYF *exits.*
ANNE *enters.*
KATHRYN *prostrates herself. So does* GEOFFREY. WILLIAM *decides against it then feels at fault and prostrates himself.* ANNE *comes through.* GEOFFREY *has rehearsed his exhortation.*

GEOFFREY: Sweet Queen, gracious light of our darkness, lustre of our eye, blush of our cheek, most precious jewel in the crown, receive our humble greetings.

KATHRYN: Majesty. First woman of our realm and fairest. 'Tis our finest hour to find your favour.

ALICE (*gleefully*): 'Tis Geoffrey and Kathryn Kolve, your Royal Highness.

KATHRYN (*hissing*): Le Kolve.

ALICE (*gleefully*): Forgive me, I still think of you as plain Kolve. I forget you have added a Le. Aye, *Le* Kolve, Majesty, of the painters' trade.

ANNE: To your feet, madam. I cannot curtsy for my head confounds me somewhat. And you, sir. My husband will receive you in the upper storey. I will walk with your wife. (*To* ALICE:) Mistress Le Kolve has written inviting us to view the pageant from her room. 'Twas a bright note and I will see it.

KATHRYN: Madam, we are delirious with joy.

ANNE: I hope not; else us both will wobble on the other to your house.

KATHRYN: Should I send for a horse, Majesty?

ALICE (*smugly*): No, mistress, the Queen likes not to ride.

ANNE (*to* ALICE): Thank you, Madam Mayor. I should like to ride this once. (*To* KATHRYN:) Come madam. (*To* GEOFFREY:) Sir, get you to my husband. (*To* WILLIAM:) Mayor, you could rise, perhaps and lead your friend to the King. *Adieu.*

KATHRYN: *Adieu* husband. Sir. Madam.

ANNE *and* KATHRYN *exit.*

WILLIAM (*brusquely*): This way, sir.

GEOFFREY: Thank you, Mister. (*To* ALICE:) Madam.

ALICE (*as the men exit*): 'Tis good the Queen came to your house at this hour. She will see it gets little sun past midday.

GEOFFREY: True, madam, little glare to distract from the plays.

. GEOFFREY *and* WILLIAM *exit.*

Scene Six

KATHRYN LE KOLVE's *bedroom.*
KATHRYN *enters with* ANNE. ANNE *inspects the bed.*

KATHRYN: Here is the room, my lady, quite nice glass; and a view, you know. Quite a nice view. We think so.

ANNE: 'Tis a marvellous bed, mistress.

KATHRYN: Aye, Majesty, much cherished.

ANNE: Has been my choice of gift since I have been to York. I have four.

KATHRYN: Five, my lady.

ANNE: Splendid!

The lights cross-fade to the Pageant House.

Scene Seven

Outside the Pageant House.
The original cast of the crucifixion play sit brooding on the news of their substitution.

EDWARD: And can they undo us so easy?

WILL: They can do what they will.

EDWARD: 'Tain't really a guild play if none of the guild be in it.

WILL: Never has been a guild play in that case. We're hardly guild. The masters is the guild not us, and they walks before the wagon or lords it from their window. We're doers. No more. Took me a bugger to learn them changes.

EDWARD: So you is to be Christ then, Walter?

WALTER: 'Tis broached but not agreed.

THOMAS: Aye, well, good luck to you Walter. I'm not grudged. You learned us our parts each year. No need to have done that then, nor feel badly now. Besides, I know they laugh at my fat Christ.

SARAH: No, they don't.

WILL: Course they don't laugh. And no, ain't your fault Walter. The King stir up nonsense in the town. Each gentleman fears disfavour, each outwits himself so as not to be outwitted by others. So 'tis a town on a sudden of no wits, no beds and a thousand wipes. Makes me spew.

SARAH: 'Tis not the King.

WILL: Course it is! 'Tis the same Richard who pissed on our dads fifteen year ago.

SARAH: Fifteen year ago, Will Bluefront, he were a boy and others ruled in his name.

WILL: 'Tis not what I heard.

SARAH: Aye, but you heard last year the Frenchies had landed and that there were a third pope.

WILL: 'Tis known history, mistress, that the King went back on his word to the commoners.

WALTER: Aye! In that case 'twill be known history that in thirteen hundred and ninety two we were replaced to improve the play. Is that right?

WILL: Improve? Bugger off!

WALTER: Why then?

WILL: 'Cause the masters is bloody dense is why.

EDWARD: Walter's right. Say why we've been chucked off Will.

WILL: Well, we knows why . . . 'tis a fever in the town, 'tis brain pox. (*He can't think, frustrated.*) I can't say in one go, why.

WALTER: An' I'm saying 'tis as likely what happened in the past to the King is as little to do with him being good or bad as us being good or bad now.

WILL: Not *us*, nipper. *You're* all right.

WALTER: I'll not do the play without you.

WILL: Ach!

SARAH (*delighted with* WALTER): Oh Walter! And nor I will.

WILL: Well, you should.

EDWARD: Course you should. Some of us should be up there.

WALTER: Besides . . . these players from Hull . . . They're rogues who do no honest labour but simply antic and clown for the big houses.

THOMAS: And I'll certain not have Sarah mingle with them.

SARAH: Nor will Sarah have Sarah mingle with them.

WALTER: Well, there you are. We're out.

SARAH: I will not hear the King blamed, sir, nor the Queen. They perceive the queue of flatterers no less than we do and have been gracious to me in this stay.

WILL: I still says is not *our* King any more than, now, is our play.

EDWARD: Course he ain't for us. An' why should he be? The shark is not for the sprat, Will. No, we is for him. Least I am. And proud of it.

WILL: Edward, you're proud of every cursed thing. You're proud of that Minster spire though will kill you and your kin in the making.

EDWARD: Aye, it will. And it will outlive us, just as the King's name will.

WILL: Ah but *he* won't, Edward. He'll be in the Dance of Death with the like of us and Master Le Kolve and the others. We'll all dance and none will be excused nor substituted.

EDWARD: And what's that got to do with our pageant? I've sulked sufficient, I'm to bed, me, and meet at Le Kolve's station for the *Corpus Christi*.

WILL: Oh no! I'm not viewing that play. Sod it!

THOMAS: Nor me.

EDWARD: Course you will. Come Thursday, you'll be jostling with the rabble and weeping at the two planks and a passion. And don't say you won't 'cause 'tis hollow threat. Nor you, Will.

WILL: Well I may. I may not.

EDWARD: Well I'll be there from the first and hope for your company. My missus still bakes her pasties and wish you share them with us.

WILL: Christ I'd quite forgot that! Can't miss them pasties and all. 'Tis a sore loss this business.

WALTER: Aye, I'll be there, Edward, but 'tis no two planks and a passion. 'Tis a new-fashioned cross and a golden Christ and a purple sea. 'Tis a spectacle . . . almost wordless.

WILL: So is our tree abandoned an' all? Ach!

WALTER: 'Tis all abandoned.

EDWARD: I've half a mind to say let's play it still.

WALTER: Do what?

EDWARD: No. I just thought.

THOMAS: I know what you thought, Edward. We could still play our old pageant and use the old gear and 'twould be no different than ever.

SARAH: To what end?

THOMAS: For our gang.

WILL: For half the town more like: who'll have no truck for golden Christs.

WALTER: Aye, but you can't push round the cross without licence.

WILL: More's the point you can't push round the cross with no wagon.

THOMAS: Then don't push it round. Play it stopped at a station.

WALTER: Whose?

THOMAS: Well . . .

SARAH: Hen Street! 'Tis not a station but could be.

THOMAS: Aye. Outside our house, eh love?

WALTER: And what of the masters? What of mine? Mr Le Kolve will not kiss me for betraying him.

WILL: 'Tis abandoned gear, we are abandoned players. If a man pick up what is thrown down 'tis no crime.

WALTER: Aye but we plan to compete.

WILL: And is competition a crime, then? In which case let the masters dungeon themselves for they will be first to gouge out their own eyes rather than be beaten to it by another. Does not your master undercut mine? Aye, he do, and so we shall play our play more cheaply and bid for the louder hurrah. I'm for it. What of the rest of you?

THOMAS: Aye, I'm game.

WILL: Edward?

EDWARD: I s'pose 'tis no great injury. The King will not view it, nor the Mayor nor Mr Le Kolve. 'Twill only be our gang.

WILL: Then 'tis up to you, Walter.

WALTER: Must I still speak for the Blessed Virgin?

WILL: Aye. And I'll scrape your jaw myself.

WALTER: Then I'll do it, but only for the pasties.

Scene Eight

The Mayor's house. The bedroom.
  ANNE is in bed. RICHARD, anxious, sleepless, presides over her. She wakes, coughs.

ANNE: Sir, did you sleep well?

RICHARD: Aye, love, and you?

ANNE: Mmm.

RICHARD: Madam 'tis capital to perjure a King.

ANNE: I said mmm. Mmm can mean many things.

RICHARD: As: no I did not sleep well but did fever and cry out and tremble so this bed did shudder.

ANNE: Then you spoke not truly to me, sir. For 'tis not well slept to catch these things.

RICHARD: Mistress. You should be attended by some physician.

ANNE: I'll have my mother and my own doctor.

RICHARD: They are not here. And they both offend you. Your mother cannot forgive you for your quiet womb and your physic cannot cure you of it.

ANNE: I chewed on Mrs Le Kolve's herbs for my belly, but 'twere a penance.

RICHARD: I should return you to London.

ANNE: But will be surrender then, not triumph.

RICHARD: I am confident, sweet, that the maggots there grow shrivelled for want of their apple and will wriggle well enough for his return. We have sent for hint of how the mood prospers. All being well we should return shortly.

ANNE: 'Tis all being *not* well presses us to.

RICHARD: No, madam, 'tis also true I am weary of gaming with these people, and could not make my home here. They come too early to fortune and choke on it.

ANNE: But if we return, what of Robert?

RICHARD: Madam, rest today, I command it. Tomorrow is the play and a darling day for us.

ANNE: If I rest what of you, husband?

RICHARD: Oh, Robert and me may ride nearby and bathe or hawk a little.

ANNE: Or wench a little.

RICHARD: Or wench a little. Aye, you has a stallion's image of me, I would not lose it. And you, do your lovers scale the walls as soon as I depart?

ANNE: In droves, sir. 'Tis an army. No wonder I tremble.

OXFORD (*off*): Majesties?

RICHARD: Robert?

OXFORD (*off*): Aye.

RICHARD: Then enter.

OXFORD: Sire, there is news from London.

RICHARD: They want me? See, I said. The cultures still have need of bits to peck at. Well, they must ransom me.

OXFORD: 'Tis from your uncle. He says the Archbishop returns to York for the *Corpus Christi.*

RICHARD: To what end?

OXFORD: I know not the motive, my Lord.

RICHARD: Does my uncle ask for my return?

OXFORD: He speak of the possibility.

RICHARD: The possibility! He speak of the possibility! I am King and there is possibility I return to my own court!

ANNE: My Lord.

OXFORD: He reports the Mayor and Sheriffs will welcome you back on certain conditions.

RICHARD: I will not hear of conditions. Conditions is weather and God have control of that and also makes Kings and subjects. Bear back to my uncle, the Regent, that my weather include need of changes, of gales, which will shiver the Mayor and his herd.

OXFORD: Should I not, instead, report your thanks and gratitude?

RICHARD: No sir! Report as I command.

OXFORD: 'Tis my experience, sir, that a spit from great distance is no match for a dagger on embracing.

RICHARD: Robert why placate me when 'tis their crew who require your absence from home, and when this chaplain arrives to poison our leisure here?

OXFORD: No. Not poison. Spice.

RICHARD: How spice?

OXFORD: Majesty, the Archbishop wants crusades and war against the French pope. He wants funds for his own knights. He will not welcome this excess on the pageants. Tomorrow will be merry with bluster from both sides.

ANNE: Aye. You should join in, sweet, and make fuss of the spectacle, saying if York be so fat – then should gift more to the nation's purse.

There is a pause.

RICHARD: 'Tis two rogues I love.

ANNE: And who love you.

RICHARD: Aye, report to my uncle our thanks and gratitude. Aye. And let us tramp outdoor today and leave the Queen to her bedfellows. 'Tis, after all, a fine day, and if I am still un-Kinged I should enjoy the summer like any citizen of the realm.

OXFORD: You will not come with us, Lady?

ANNE: I grow such a connoisseur of beds, Robert. I must savour them all day.

RICHARD: The Queen thinks we hunt for maids and not for fish.

OXFORD: Then let's promise to cook whatever we catch and supper on it.

ANNE: Best make it young girl then, Robert. Richard says my flesh is tough now.

RICHARD: Tough? 'Tis unchewable. I'll show you. (*He kisses* ANNE.) Adieu, madam, and be waited on.

ANNE: Aye, sir, and you escape from worry . . . Adieu Robert.

OXFORD: Adieu Majesty.

RICHARD: I'll send in your woman.

> RICHARD *and* OXFORD *exit.*
> ANNE *alone, coughs violently and pulls the covers over her head.*

Scene Nine

Downstairs in the Mayor's house.
> OXFORD *and* RICHARD *prepare for their outing.*

OXFORD: So, you'll go back?

RICHARD: Aye, we'll submit. If only to get the Queen to her physic.

OXFORD: Aye, 'tis reason enough. And I'll go back after tomorrow. I'll take a horse and ride cross country. Then a boat to Ireland.

RICHARD: I'll go to Ireland in the autumn! We could meet.

OXFORD (*doubtfully*): Mmmm.

RICHARD: Except I may be more King then. And chaperoned.

OXFORD: Well . . .

RICHARD: More King and less Queen. She will not see September but see God first.

OXFORD: Come now . . .

RICHARD: No, 'tis fact. She has the most alive mind I know and the least alive body. The one seems to suck out the other too quick.

OXFORD: She may improve. These things are uncertain.

RICHARD: A new Queen is already arranged for me . . . not yet seven years old. I must be widowed then ringed to a baby. 'Tis a black prospect.

OXFORD: Then do not remarry.

RICHARD: Oh, Robert, we have an innocent eye of the world. 'Tis a machine and the King is but one cog and no more able to stop its workings than any other. 'Tis a great windmill and will grind us all. I am married to produce . . . to father . . . they give me a new womb to work at, once I have buried my grievance with the city – and buried the woman I love. Then, bereaved of dignity and bereaved of heart, I can stud and be put out to pasture.

OXFORD: This is bleak, my Lord. We promised to escape from worry. Where would you go?

RICHARD: To the country, sir. To the forest.

OXFORD: Aye. To forest fires, Richard, and warm, fat, forest haunches. Let's tumble off these humours – let's paddle. Let's baste ourselves.

RICHARD: Oh, sir. I want air, not smothering, not smothering.

OXFORD: Then let's have air, Majesty. Air all day.

RICHARD: Aye, but fun tomorrow, eh? There is still a little juice left in these York lemons. Let's squeeze out the last drop.

OXFORD: I never tasted a lemon.

RICHARD: I was sent six from the Roman pope.

OXFORD: What were they like?

RICHARD: Well, he also sent sugar. Sugar is better.

OXFORD: Aye, I like sugar.

RICHARD: I have some with me. Shall we taste it?

OXFORD: Aye.

RICHARD *produces a handkerchief. The sugar is wrapped inside.*

RICHARD: 'Tis milled fine.

RICHARD *licks his finger and dips it. Then he offers some to* OXFORD *who does the same.*

Scene Ten

The upstairs window of the Mayor's house looking out onto the street.

The idea is that the light on RICHARD *and* OXFORD *in their cups fades to black and this new one flashes up broad Midsummer's Day and noisy and the start of the* Corpus Christi *cycle. There are about forty-eight plays in the cycle. The Mayor's play is number nineteen, the Le Kolves', number thirty-five. What happens is that there are twelve stations . . . Le Kolves' perhaps the fourth in order and the Mayor's about eighth. Each play plays all twelve stations; the wagon being pulled from station to station. This all takes a considerable amount of time. It's unlikely that the cycle was completed within the twenty-four hours . . . It would be mid-afternoon by the time the Herod play was viewed by anyone and practically midnight for the Crucifixion. The late plays, therefore, were lit by torches: an expensive business. Great care would be taken to ensure the plays moved swiftly and efficiently: any traffic jam would have drastic consequences.*

The scene starts about seven in the morning at the latest, with the ARCHBISHOP, *the* MAYOR *and* MAYORESS *up at the window as the Creation Play, play number one, is waiting to start outside.* KATHRYN *and* GEOFFREY LE KOLVE, *with* FATHER MELTON, *are ready at the* LE KOLVE's *window. There would be a huge crowd at each station. The upstairs window above the play is, of course, reserved for the fat cats . . . it's the box at the opera. The play is held up for the arrival of* KING, QUEEN, *and* OXFORD. *This does not please the* ARCHBISHOP. *The* SELBYS *attempt to mediate.*

ALICE (*anxious*): Will you eat more, my lord Archbishop?

ARCHBISHOP (*accepting, eating*): Hmm. 'Tis good your pie goes down well with me this morning, Mrs. For nothing else do.

ALICE: Thank you, my lord.

ARCHBISHOP: Aye, 'tis a fat pie. But then 'tis a fat family. Indeed I come back to York and I am struck by fat. Everywhere fat.

ALICE (*mortified*): Oh.

ARCHBISHOP: I hear your play is fat, mayor.

WILLIAM: Well . . .

ARCHBISHOP: Yes, fat everywhere. There is surely a connection between God and fat . . . so much God, so much fat. More of one means less of the other. Let's have less fat, mayor. Eh? Eh?

WILLIAM: Right.

ARCHBISHOP: Ach! The plays must begin. I think someone really should tell his Majesty that 'tis one thing to miss Holy Mass this morning, 'tis quite another to miss the Creation of the World.

WILLIAM (*acutely embarrassed and distressed*): 'Tis said he rouses, my Lord.

ARCHBISHOP: Oh marvellous! The miracle of Genesis and the miracle of his appearance all at once.

ALICE: We understand the Majesties slept not well.

ARCHBISHOP: Madam I push in thistles to my mattress to ensure I sleep not well. To sleep heavy is a venial sin, in my opinion.

ALICE (*to* WILLIAM): Should we call down to hold up the start?

ARCHBISHOP: Aye! Hold up Creation. Good idea. (*Hugely and crassly.*) Hold up down there! We wait on the King.

> *Dissenting murmurs are heard from below.*
> OXFORD *enters blearily.*

OXFORD: The King approaches. (*He sees the* ARCHBISHOP.) Good morning, my lord.

ARCHBISHOP: Is it the Earl of Oxford?

OXFORD: Aye.

ARCHBISHOP: I am amazed, sir. The law exiled you, surely?

OXFORD: From London.

ARCHBISHOP: Oh no, sir. 'Twas from the realm.

OXFORD: The whole realm? Then I should not be here.

ARCHBISHOP: No sir, you should not.

OXFORD: 'Tis remarkable. The King and me both thought it were banished from London and the gaze of the new muscle.

ARCHBISHOP: No, I seen the papers as witness. An' 'tis not new muscle. 'Tis simply muscle long unflexed.

OXFORD: I'd best be off soon then. To somewhere deeply foreign.

ARCHBISHOP: Aye, deeply foreign were best, sir.

OXFORD: How is your hair shirt, my Lord?

ARCHBISHOP: Installed. (*He pulls at his clothes to reveal it.*)

OXFORD: Ah, there she is! I hear you wear it even when you take pleasure. That, to me, is the sign of a saintly man.

ARCHBISHOP: You missed the Mass this morning my Lord. 'Tis a mortal sin.

OXFORD: Oh I think we'll find a Mass somewhere later on. Surely?

> RICHARD *and* ANNE *appear,* ANNE *fragile,* RICHARD *hungover.*

ARCHBISHOP: Majesty. (*To* ANNE:) Majesty.

RICHARD: My Lord Archbishop. This is a most pleasant surprise.

ARCHBISHOP: Ah, if you did not expect me, Majesty, then I am understood why you attended not my Mass and sermon.

RICHARD: No, Lord, we knew of your presence in the town but not of your presence at the Mayor's window. I like not to be told off before the plays and will have Mass later and without preaching.

RICHARD *walks to the window. Applause is heard. He and* ANNE *wave.*

RICHARD: That's a good crowd, eh mayor? Not bad at all. (*Shouting down:*) Do start! (*Then back to* MAYORESS:) Any more pie? His Grace seems to have hogged all ours.

God the Father appears, if possible from a high point in the theatre corresponding to a high point in the street: say an arch of the city walls or a bell tower, to begin the first play, with dazzling light behind him, so as practically to obscure his face (which is a gold mask)
The constant murmur and humour of the crowd dies away to reverence as the character speaks. There is genuine excitement.

GOD: *Ego sum alpha and O, vita, via, veritas,*
           Primus et Novissimus.
           I am gracious and great, God without a
           beginning; I am maker unmade and all might is in me.

ANNE (*clapping her hands*): Oh, I love a good God!

* * * * *

Later. The LE KOLVES' *station.*
KATHRYN, GEOFFREY, SARAH *and* FATHER MELTON *watch the explosive Herod play;* JOLYF *is doing his stuff below.*

JOLYF: No noise nippers. What!
           Who dares mutter when I appear?
           Herod – the mighty, marvellous, perfect.
           Who dares talk
           when such magnificence come to York!
           I bluster and blast. I blow and blunder.
           I crackle and clap and grunt and thunder.
           I am most terrible, me!
           Point out a man who is not on his knee
           and I'll snap off his legs like twigs off a tree.

KATHRYN (*enjoying this hugely*): Gross. Ugh!

FATHER MELTON: 'Tis a reaction cheaply bought.

KATHRYN: Do Herod fart? I remember it not from the scripture.

FATHER MELTON: The mask is very fine, though, Mister.

GEOFFREY: Aye, 'tis too fine a mask for the player.

SARAH: 'Tis Walter's face, Madam. He made it.

KATHRYN: Did he? Aye, 'tis well done.

GEOFFREY: Where is Walter! He were bidden aloft.

SARAH: Uh. He stays with the others of the old pageant.

GEOFFREY (*miffed*): Does he? Hmm. (*To* KATHRYN:) What time is the King due?

KATHRYN (*watching despite herself*): Sssh!

GEOFFREY: Sssh not! Beside, the rabble makes so much din the play can hardly be heard.

KATHRYN: Sssh!

FATHER MELTON: I think Mister, he is sure to wait until this play is done outside the Mayor's station. This will not be until mid-afternoon.

KATHRYN: Later.

GEOFFREY: Should we wait on our feast, though?

KATHRYN (*not looking at him but with half an ear on the conversation*): Husband, we cannot eat before the Royalty arrives.

GEOFFREY: Madam, our play will not be here until near midnight. If the King deigns not to enter prior to then, our diet will be too much play, too little food.

KATHRYN: Oh, he will, he must. Sssh. For heaven's sake.

GEOFFREY: This King will or must do nothing.

FATHER MELTON: Aye. 'Tis true. He attended not the Archbishop's Mass this morning.

GEOFFREY: We heard he were discovered sleeping with the Queen, Oxford and a horse in his bed.

KATHRYN: Sssh, please. May not be well done, but 'tis a marvellous story all the same.

*   *   *   *   *

Later, outside the Selby station. JOLYF *has reached his patron's station. He elaborates and explodes hugely.*

JOLYF: Not just Richard come to rest
               but three more Kings from East and West arrive with word
               of some nipper born in a stable
               meant to be saviour, meant to be able to save the world.
               No bairn from a barn will compete with me.
               I am the biggest and blackest and cruellest and meanest.

Upstairs RICHARD *and* OXFORD *and* ANNE *misbehave. They are at the cold buffet at this most inauspicious time. The Selbys are increasingly desperate to get them to watch.*

WILLIAM (*proudly*): This be our pageant, my Lord.

RICHARD: Who's your man?

WILLIAM: He's imported sir.

RICHARD (*mischievously*): Shame.

WILLIAM: Exceptional red hair on him.

RICHARD (*mischievously*): 'Tis a wig though, surely.

WILLIAM (*defeated*): Uh.

RICHARD: The man at Coventry had most marvellous hair. (*Wandering off.*) Anne, are you drinking?

OXFORD: This one has most marvellous arse!

ARCHBISHOP: I cannot hear, sir.

OXFORD: The arse? Why, sir, it explodes noisily.

ARCHBISHOP: The play!

RICHARD: Who's hungry?

WILLIAM: My Lord, we thought to eat *after* the play!

ARCHBISHOP: 'Tis very broad this show and foul.

WILLIAM: Uh.

ARCHBISHOP: 'Tis not meet to inflate Herod so.

OXFORD: Why's that, my Lord?

ARCHBISHOP: These pageants give too much air to evil and insufficient to good.

ALICE: Well, surely Lord, the evil parts is best fun.

ARCHBISHOP: Madam, 'tis the feast of Christ's Body, not a funfair.

WILLIAM *and* ALICE *are upset that nobody watches the play which continues during this dispute.*

OXFORD: Aye, Reverend, but a pageant of Christ and Mary and Angels would send the rabble asleep.

ARCHBISHOP: That's blasphemy, sir.

OXFORD (*enjoying himself hugely*): No, 'tis fact. A fact cannot be blasphemy, can it?

WILLIAM: Please sir, you miss the play!

RICHARD: I know. (*To* ALICE:) 'Tis your cooking, madam. 'Tis a temptation. Robert, you should taste this chicken!

ALICE (*hysterically*): No! Please! Watch the play! Please!

ARCHBISHOP: In my opinion, these plays grow annually more vulgar. 'Tis a procession of guts and violence and lewd laughter. 'Twere the subject of my message this morning.

RICHARD: And we missed it.

ALICE (*frustrated*): Sirs, he made reference to the King.

RICHARD: Who?

ALICE: The Herod.

RICHARD: The Herod? What reference?

ALICE: He mentioned Your Majesty and the town.

RICHARD: Did he? And we missed that an' all. Can he repeat it?

ALICE: Uh.

ANNE: Why?

ALICE: Why? Madam?

ANNE: Aye, why?

ALICE: Why what?

ANNE: Why did the Herod mention my husband?

ALICE: Uh . . . (*To* WILLIAM:) Why, husband?

WILLIAM: Out of topicality.

RICHARD: Oh, topicality! Did he mention my Lord the Archbishop?

WILLIAM: Uh. I don't recall.

RICHARD (*impishly*): You're not mentioned, my Lord. Not topical enough.

ARCHBISHOP: I cannot follow this play for the buzz up here.

OXFORD: Buzz? Who buzzes? Do you buzz my lady?

ARCHBISHOP: The din you make, my Lord!

OXFORD:
RICHARD: Oh, the din, the din!
ANNE:

WILLIAM: My Lords, please! 'Tis the killing of the babes to come.

Below, JOLYF *continues.*

JOLYF: I am the biggest and blackest and cruellest and meanest.
                   I've sent out soldiers to scour the town
                   and butcher all brats to bits and pieces. Tomorrow I'll
                   breakfast on babby bacon and childy chops and smoked nipper
                   and infant pie and guarantee that come tonight there'll be no
                   tiny Messiah. There'll be no star in the sky.
                   There'll only be me, horrible Herod,
                   There'll only be myself, there'll only be I!

                   Herod's soldiers splash the guts of the butchered babies. The
                   ARCHBISHOP *is flecked.*

ARCHBISHOP: By Christ! I am all a-bloodied.

OXFORD: You are, my Lord. Your ermine looks freshly killed.

ARCHBISHOP: Ach!

ALICE: I sicken sir.

WILLIAM (*in despair*): Oh, madam!

ANNE: Oh dear!

WILLIAM: Oh God. Don't swoon, please.

ANNE: I think she do, Mister.

ALICE *faints.*

OXFORD: Aye. There she goes.

ARCHBISHOP: Is there mess on my face?

OXFORD: Um. (*He inspects gravely.*) 'Tis hard to say, Lord.

ARCHBISHOP: I must go in and clean myself. Ach!

WILLIAM (*abjectly*): My Lord, you'll miss the play.

ARCHBISHOP: Would it had missed me, sir!

The ARCHBISHOP *exits, flicking imaginary blood from his clothes.*
                                    * * * * *

Minutes to midnight, back at the impatient LE KOLVES'.

GEOFFREY (*funereally*): 'Tis our play next madam.

KATHRYN: Some minutes off.

GEOFFREY: Some minutes! The day is finished and no King. How much later can
    he be and not miss it?

KATHRYN: Some minutes. Sarah has fetched them. Calm yourself.

GEOFFREY: Do you know the bill of the play?

KATHRYN: Aye, you said.

GEOFFREY: God's teeth. And I starve madam!

KATHRYN: You had food earlier.

GEOFFREY: 'Twould not fill a rabbit.

KATHRYN: Sir, more will spoil your feast. Shut up now.

FATHER MELTON: Sir, we are in good stead. Each pageant processes, none to rival ours. 'Tis a triumph. Our crowd is vast and high spirited and will hurrah us.

This signals a cheer from below.

GEOFFREY (*in a voice of doom, looking out and down the street*): See! 'Tis our pageant.

KATHRYN: Is it?

GEOFFREY: Aye, madam. It comes.

KATHRYN: Bother.

GEOFFREY: *It* comes but the King comes not. 'Tis wasted. (*He sits down.*) Ach! (*Muttering.*) Blessed Virgin Mary, Mother of God. 'Tis complete wasted. 'Tis money melted. 'Tis harvest rotted. 'Tis feast unfeasted. I said this would happen. God, God, God.

KATHRYN: I bet 'tis the Mayor. I see his hand in this, or his shrew. They sulk so miserable after their flat affair they cannot bear the King to see ours. Witch!

FATHER MELTON: Can we not send horses?

GEOFFREY: We can send nothing with the wagons cramming the roads.

KATHRYN: Then we'll wait.

GEOFFREY: Can't.

KATHRYN: We can. We says 'Wait!' and they wait.

GEOFFREY: 'Tis an offence and will be fined: six shillings and eight pence.

KATHRYN: Then we will be fined but the King will see the play.

GEOFFREY: The additional torches?

KATHRYN: Sir, we are in danger of losing everything and you carp at torches!

GEOFFREY: Do you know the price of a torch, madam?

KATHRYN: Please don't tell me.

GEOFFREY: We paid Margaret Chandler fourteen shillings for six.

KATHRYN: Will you cry wait to them?

GEOFFREY: Ach.

KATHRYN: Then *I* will, and I'll barge through the throng also to fetch this King. Since no one else offer. If you want something doing, Kathryn, do it yourself.

KATHRYN *stomps off.*

Scene Eleven

The Streets.
The Royal party walk with SARAH *to the* LE KOLVES' *house. It is dark and in the distance light and noise come from the various stations.*

SARAH: Sir, we must hurry.

RICHARD: Must we?

SARAH: Aye. That were the pageant before the Cross play we passed.

ANNE: Aye, Richard, let's be swift. 'Tis my favourite and has Sarah's husband in it. He do the Christ.

SARAH: No, he don't madam. They've changed the crew.

ANNE: Oh?

SARAH: Aye. To flatter you. They have foreign players. They have a maid to play the Mary.

OXFORD: A woman?

SARAH: Aye. They wanted me.

OXFORD: Well, that's novel. Is she pretty?

SARAH: She comes from Hull.

OXFORD: Aye, but do she come prettily from Hull?

ANNE: Sir, hold up a second. (*She coughs and holds her side.*)

RICHARD: Madam?

ANNE *coughs violently.*

ANNE: God. (*She sinks down to the ground.*)

OXFORD: Majesty, do you sicken?

ANNE: Aye. (*She coughs into her handkerchief. It comes away from her mouth bloodied.*)

SARAH: Oh ma'am, you bleed!

ANNE: Aye, it seem so.

SARAH: My Lord. There is my house nearby. 'Tis poor but you are welcome to rest up there awhile. And . . . you could watch the old Cross play . . . if you wished to. My husband's boys play it there for their own gang.

ANNE: I'd like that. Richard.

RICHARD: Let's to it. We'll carry you, darling.

ANNE: Aye and get me to a bed, sir.

RICHARD (*worried*): Madam you are a devil for a bed.

SARAH: This way, my Lord.

They struggle off.

Scene Twelve

The LE KOLVES' *house.*
The position of the house has changed so that now we see less front on and therefore beyond the house catch a glimpse of the new wagon complete, in the flickering torchlight, with all-gold Christ. Acres of purple and some soldiers hanging around waiting to begin. There are restless sounds from the unseen crowd.
GEOFFREY *is suicidal at the window. There is a noise below.*
WILLIAM *and the* ARCHBISHOP *enter angrily.*

WILLIAM: Mister, what is the meaning of this delay? The wagons jam up behind.

GEOFFREY: We wait on the King, sir.

WILLIAM: The King? The King left my house an hour ago to join you.

GEOFFREY: He come not.

ARCHBISHOP: This King needs no fool to entertain him. He do the job for himself. 'Tis an outrage.

WILLIAM: By Christ, our day is poxed by his manners and we are the laughing stock, sir. He yapped, him and his two dogs, throughout our pageant and now will dodge yours altogether.

ARCHBISHOP: Aye, Mister.

WILLIAM: No more. Go ahead, sir.

GEOFFREY (*adamant*): I'll not. The King must view the play.

WILLIAM: The King, Mister, may be in Coventry for all we know.

GEOFFREY: Sir, has broken us, the brunt of this pageant and the King *must* view it. There's a gold Christ and a purple sea.

ARCHBISHOP: A gold Christ. 'Tis inappropriate. 'Tis pagan.

FATHER MELTON: Oh no, my Lord, 'tis majestic.

ARCHBISHOP: 'Tis unchristian, Parson. We'll have sacrifices next.

WILLIAM: We'll have the play next and now. Or I'll call in the sergeants . . The rabble boil and are all end-o-day shirty and hackled. There'll be a Carlisle axe swung before long unless they gets their pageant.
        KATHRYN *and* ALICE *enter.*

KATHRYN: Husband, order the play started.

GEOFFREY: Do the King appear?

KATHRYN: He does not, sir, but our old pageant starts up outside a private station.

GEOFFREY: What's that?

KATHRYN: The men from the play, your apprentice and gang, make the old pageant. Now our play play not, the crowd wander down to view it. Soon will be deserted below.

ALICE: 'Tis a devil, this business, and I sorrow for you, mistress.

KATHRYN: Thank you, my Lady. I love your wipe. Is it silk?

ALICE: Aye, a little silk. Our day is spoiled an' all. And I've swooned.

KATHRYN: Dear Madam, friend Mayor, my Lord, let's view the pageant severally. King or no King.

ALICE: Thank you madam.

WILLIAM: My Lord, the Archbishop, tells us this is the colour of his Majesty. Unworthy of the crown. Our brothers in London know it and work on it.

GEOFFREY: Do they? (*To* KATHRYN:) I smelled that from the off.

WILLIAM: Aye and we should learn, eh, Archbishop?

ARCHBISHOP: You should.

WILLIAM: So sit eh? And be peaceful.

ARCHBISHOP: Is there blood in this pageant?

FATHER MELTON: None, my Lord. 'Tis a serene cross.

ARCHBISHOP: Well that's something.

KATHRYN: Do we start then husband?

GEOFFREY: Aye, we start. Go to, down there, and begin.

The crowd roar their approval. Trumpets sound. The burghers, ominously united, hold their handkerchiefs aloft, waving them like banners.

Scene Thirteen

Hen Street. A hut.
    ANNE *is in* SARAH's *bed.* RICHARD *sits by her.* SARAH *and* OXFORD *stand facing front half-watching the play: the old Cross play. In the background throughout the new Pageant proceeds, illuminated from time to time by a torch which shows the golden Christ crucified, then later the ubiquitous purple sea.*

ANNE: I am feeble, sir.

RICHARD: You're drained, sweet, 'tis too long a day and too much sport.

ANNE: Aye.

RICHARD: How's the bed?

ANNE: Oh. Fine.

RICHARD: Best bed?

ANNE: Most welcome, sir.

RICHARD: Then sleep, eh love?

ANNE (*regretfully*): I miss the passion play.

RICHARD: Aye. 'Tis a rough and ready one proceed outside.

ANNE: Can I not view it?

RICHARD: Madam, you can sleep.

ANNE: I can sleep later.

RICHARD: Robert?

OXFORD: Aye, my Lord?

RICHARD: How is the play?

OXFORD: Humble, sir. Very special.

RICHARD: Then help me drag the Queen's bed to the doorway.

OXFORD: Aye, most willingly.

    RICHARD *and* OXFORD *drag the bed down to the doorway.*

RICHARD: Can you see, my lady?

ANNE: Almost.

RICHARD (*helping* ANNE, *gently*): Let's plump up more cushion. There.

ANNE: Aye! I can see now: oh, the Christ have a fine leg on him.

OXFORD: Aye, he do.

SARAH: 'Tis my husband, madam.

ANNE (*smiling weakly*): Is it, Sarah? I like a nice Christ.

RICHARD: Madam, this is the most dilute apology to spend your life in bed.

ANNE: Shut up, Richard.

RICHARD: Must I take you back to London still in it?

ANNE: Aye. Come you both, sit by me, 'tis a fine view.

    They watch. And with them we hear the climax of the Crucifixion.

CHRIST (THOMAS): . . . your son swoons dear Lord
                    And I pray
                    That all that I suffer may not be in vain
                    But bring down your mercy on men
                    Like an endless cleansing rain.

MARY (WALTER): Alas, my love, my life, my Liege.
      Alas, mourning now maddens me.
      Alas, my boy look down on me.
      Thy mother that did bear thee.
      You are my fruit. I fostered thee,
      And gave thee suck upon my knee.
      Upon my pain have pity.
      Alas to find my boy above me
      Tugged! Lugged! Broken! Tree'd!
      Nails thrust in and crowned of thorns.
      To see my birth that I have born, bleed:
      Tears my heart to tatters.
      And though you hang above me, wracked on high
      I, at the tree's foot, am also crucified.

OXFORD (*after a moment*): You're weeping, madam.

ANNE: I do, Robert. I always forget, 'tis such a cruel play.

THE END

Appendix

Expanded Herod play.

Depending on the production it might prove expedient to have additional text for the Herod and his gang to cover proceedings at the two households.

HEROD:
No noise, nippers. What!
Who dares mutter when I appear?
Herod, the mighty, marvellous, perfect.
Who dares talk when such magnificence come to York!
I bluster and blast, I blow and thunder.
I am most terrible, me.
Point out a man who is not on his knee and I'll snap off his legs
like twigs off a tree.
Point out a man who carps of a King:
I'll pull off his skin
roast his carcass, you'll see.
I'll not have noise of some brat in a cradle
I'll not have nonsense of stars and fables
I'll not tolerate talk of a Messiah . . .
Did anyone say Messiah?
Was the word Messiah whispered?
Or Emmanuel? Or Son of God. I hope not.
And kings. Everywhere kings.
A man cannot walk Mickelgate without bumping
Kings. Are you a King? Bash his bonce.
Not just Richard come to rest.
but three more kings from East and West
arrive with word of some nipper, born in a stable
Meant to be able to save the world.
No bairn from a barn can compete with me!
I am the biggest and blackest and cruellest
and meanest.
I am fattest and foulest and filthy uncleanest!
I am dazzlingly bad! I am evil. I'm mad!
I make grown men weep, I make babies screech.
I make mothers tremble. I am gurt bad!
And I hate hearing of Messiahs.
I hate the word Messiah.
I hate it, it hurts, I'll clap the next bugger
who mumbles Messiah. I don't like the word.

SERVANT:
Sir, there's noise of a nipper just born.
Full of light, yet unadorned.
Born with nothing, under a star
followed by kings from off as far as Egypt
and France and Belgium and Wakefield and
Norway. All these kings will bow down it's said.
To this bairn in a stable
Born with the moon and stars on his head.
Tis a marvellous thing and the joy spreads like fire.
From every house all over York:
Messiah! Messiah! Messiah! Messiah!

HEROD:
I've sent out soldiers to scour the town.
And butcher all brats to bits and pieces.

Tomorrow I'll breakfast on babby bacon and
childy chops and smoked nipper and infant pie
And guarantee that come tomorrow, there'll be no
Tiny Messiah. There'll be no star in the sky.
There'll only be me, horrible Herod.
There'll only be myself. There'll only be I!

Screams and chaos as HEROD's SOLDIERS *butcher the babies and splash the guts.*

CHORUS OF WOMEN:
They've killed our boys. They've butchered them.
They've broke our hearts, our babbies slain.
Our babbies slain: they'll never cry or laugh again
or learn their names or live to learn that they must die
to save the boy who'll never die:
Messiah! Messiah! Messiah!

The CHORUS *sing the 'Sanctus'.*